EVERYDAY DOINGS OF INSECTS

British Library Cataloguing-in-Publication Data
A catalogue record for this book is available from the
British Library

EVERYDAY DOINGS
OF INSECTS

BY

EVELYN CHEESMAN F.E.S. F.Z.S.

CURATOR OF INSECTS TO THE ZOOLOGICAL SOCIETY OF LONDON

WITH ILLUSTRATIONS BY
HUGH MAIN DR HERBERT SHIRLEY PETER SCOTT
THE AUTHOR AND OTHERS

LEAF INSECT

Entomology

Entomology (from the Greek *entomos* meaning 'that which is cut in pieces or engraved/segmented', hence 'insect' and *logia,* meaning 'study') is the scientific study of insects – a branch of anthropodology.

In the past, the term 'insect' was more vague, and historically the definition of entomology included the study of terrestrial animals in other arthropod groups, such as arachnids, myriapods, earthworms, land snails, and slugs. This wider meaning may still be encountered in informal use, though generally not within the scientific community.

At some 1.3 million described species, insects account for more than two-thirds of all known organisms, date back some 400 million years, and have many kinds of interactions with humans and other forms of life on earth. Entomology is rooted in nearly all human cultures from prehistoric times, primarily in the context of agriculture, and especially in the forms of biological control and beekeeping. The earliest evidence of man's interest in insects is from rock paintings depicting bees, dating from around 13,000 BCE. These pollinating insects continued to fascinate early civilisations all over the world, and later discoveries were made of jewellery depicting bees holding a drop of honey, dated around 1800–1700 BCE in Malia, Crete.

One of the first texts on entomology was written in 1350, by Konrad of Megenberg (1309 – 1374); a German Catholic scholar and author. *Buch der Natur* was the first natural history in the German language, and contained a substantial section entitled 'Von den Würmen' – meaning, *on worms*. It also describes insects both real and imaginary, as well as reptiles. Scientific entomology only really began in the sixteenth century. Although the earliest pictorial record of a natural history cabinet is the engraving in Ferrante Imperato's *Dell'Historia Naturale* (Naples, 1599), they were little more than rudimentary collections before this date. Several beautiful illustrated works were produced however, such as the *Grand Heures of Anne of Brittany* (1503), with accurate marginal illustrations of plants and insects, and the *Animalia Rationalia et Inescta* by Joris Hoefnagel, finished in 1580.

In the eighteenth century, three kinds of entomological text appeared. Firstly there were illustrative works – showing insects often beautifully coloured whose purpose was largely sensual. An example is afforded by Maria von Merian's *Metamorphosis Insectorum Surinamenis* (1705). Second were descriptive and systematic (classificatory) works usually confined to what are now known as the Insecta. Of the second kind, Carl von Linne's *Systema Naturae,* published in 1758 at Uppsala, stands proud. In this work the binomial system was finally settled on. Thirdly were works on developmental biology (life cycles), internal anatomy, physiology and so on. These often covered other invertebrate groups. An example is René Antoine Ferchault de Réaumur's *Memoires pour Servir a L'Historie des Insectes.*

William Kirby (an English entomologist and country priest; 1759 - 1850) is widely considered as the father of Entomology. In collaboration with William Spence (1783 -

1860), he published a definitive entomological encyclopaedia, the *Introduction to Entomology*, regarded as the subject's foundational text. He also helped to found the Royal Entomological Society in London in 1833, one of the earliest such societies in the world.

Forensic entomology is also an important branch of the discipline, as the specific application and study of insect biology to criminal matters. Song Ci (also known as Sung Tz'u) was a Judicial Intendant who lived in China, and the first person to write on the subject. In 1247 CE, Song Ci wrote a book entitled *Washing Away of Wrongs* as a handbook for coroners. It is the first recorded account in history of someone using forensic entomology for judicial means, and remained uncountered until the seventeenth century. In 1668, Italian physician Francesco Redi disproved Song Ci's theory of spontaneous generation (that maggots and other insects develop spontaneously from rotting meat). This discovery completely changed the way people viewed the decomposition of organisms and prompted further investigations into insect life cycles and entomology in general.

Entomology developed rapidly in the nineteenth and twentieth centuries, and was studied by large numbers of people, including such notable figures as Charles Darwin, Jean-Henri Fabre, Vladimir Nabokov, Karl von Frisch (winner of the 1973 Nobel Prize in Physiology or Medicine), and two-time Pulitzer Prize winner E. O. Wilson. Thanks to their ground-breaking work, most insects can easily be recognized to order, such as Hymenoptera (bees, wasps, and ants) or Coleoptera (beetles). Insects other than Lepidoptera (butterflies and moths) are typically identifiable to genus or species only through the use of Identification keys and Monographs. Because the class Insecta contains a very large number of species (over 330,000 species of beetles alone) and the characteristics separating them are often unfamiliar and subtle (or invisible without a microscope), this is often very difficult even for a specialist. Such problems in entomology have led to the development of automated species identification systems targeted on insects, for example, 'Daisy', 'ABIS', 'SPIDA' and 'Draw-wing'.

Like other scientific specialties, entomologists have a number of local, national, and international organizations. There are also many organizations specializing in specific sub-areas such as the 'Amateur Entomologist's Society', the aforementioned 'Royal Entomological Society of London' (and other similar organisations across the world), as well as the 'International Union for the Study of Social Insects'. Many museums now also hold vast collections of insects, and the science has found its way into popular culture. For instance, in Arthur Conan Doyle's story, *The Hound of the Baskervilles*, the villain is a naturalist who collects butterflies, making him an 'evil' entomologist.

Aside from the world of professional entomology, insect identification is an increasingly common hobby, with butterflies and dragonflies being the most popular subjects of enquiry. As is evident from this brief introduction, it is a branch of science with an incredibly long history. The study and knowledge of insects helped our earliest ancestors survive in the harshest environments, and throughout the medieval, renaissance, and later periods, was systematised and given a proper scholarly foundation. Entomological studies continue to develop in the present day, and it is hoped that the current reader enjoys this book on the subject.

TO

ALL WHO LOVE THE INSECT HOUSE

In Nature's infinite book of secrecy a little I can read.
SHAKESPEARE

FOREWORD

THIS little book does not pretend to discuss *all* the daily events of insect life, but it is an attempt to answer a few of the questions which are constantly asked concerning the exhibits in the Insect House. They are queries which naturally arise over the everyday happenings that are taking place there under the visitors' eyes during the greater part of the year, and yet again and again when one is asked, " Where can we read of these things ? What book do you recommend ? " the unsatisfactory answer has to be given that the most thrilling truths about these wonderful little lives can be collected only from various scientific books and papers which are in the libraries of scientific societies, and therefore inaccessible to the ordinary inquirer.

It is particularly to boy inquirers that these chapters are addressed, in the ambitious hope, not indeed of sating their appetite for information, but of inducing a permanent state of voracity ; for there is surely no greater proof of a healthy mind than the thirst for information concerning the sweet, true things of nature.

The photographs and sketches have been made from the *living* insect in almost every case—except of course the diagrams—and it is because these pages are enriched by exceptionally charming studies from nature by the sympathetic hands of Mr Hugh Main, Dr Herbert Shirley, and Mr Peter Scott that the author is confident that they will appeal to all who have a real affection for the insect world. Illustrations which do not bear the name of a photographer or artist are contributed by the author.

E. C.

CONTENTS

ILLUSTRATIONS

14

ILLUSTRATIONS

15

ILLUSTRATIONS

EVERYDAY DOINGS
OF INSECTS

CHAPTER I

HOW INSECTS GROW

MOST insects hatch out of an egg ; there are a few kinds which are born alive, but they are quite an exception. The eggs are never very large, and in order to appreciate their beauty it is necessary to use a lens ; then it will be seen how much they vary in shape and colour, for an insect's egg is really a lovely object. Some have patterns on them, spots and blotches like a bird's egg ; or the pattern may be moulded as it is on stick insects' and leaf insects' eggs. They may be round, oval, or long ; and they may be flattened against the surface they are fastened to or suspended on long stalks.

The manner in which different insects place their eggs varies very much too. They may be placed singly, or glued together in clusters ; they may be wrapped up very carefully each in a separate bundle of fluff, as by some moths, or they may be dropped about carelessly on the ground, or even hurled away to a distance. Stick insects and leaf insects drop their eggs quite casually under trees and bushes wherever they happen to be feeding. This is not as careless as it might

SIX GROUPS OF MOTHS' EGGS

1. Lappet Moth.   2. Kentish Glory.   3. Oak-egger.
4. Emperor Moth.   5. Drinker Moth.   6. Fox Moth.

A. E. Tonge and Hugh Main

EGG-SHOOTING ORGAN OF GIANT STICK INSECT

appear, for these eggs are very like the seeds of plants, with hard brown outer coats and a dry appearance ; so the very place where they will be least conspicuous is on the soil, and

EGGS OF LEAF INSECT
Hugh Main

WINGLESS VAPOURER MOTH LAYING
HER EGGS
Hugh Main

EGGS OF PLANT BUG
Hugh Main

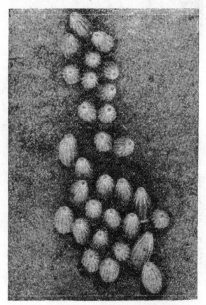

EGGS OF THE LARGE WHITE BUTTERFLY
Hugh Main

when they are ready to hatch they will be supplied with the necessary moisture to soften the shell. The females of some of the Giant Stick Insects, whose eggs are large enough to attract the undesirable attention of birds and mice, have a peculiar apparatus at the end of the body for shooting their eggs to quite a long distance. By thus scattering them in all directions they probably give the eggs a better chance of escaping destruction.

EGGS OF LACE WING FLY
CLUSTERED ON LONG STALKS
Hugh Main

Some insects' eggs are laid in holes in the ground or in crevices in the bark of trees or in the stems of plants, and in order to put them away safely the females have a special instrument (ovipositor) for boring or digging. Occasionally a case is made for the eggs, the material which forms it being produced from the female's body. Cockroaches, for instance, pack their eggs in quaint little portmanteaux, usually with patterns on them; the mother insect will carry them about for days before putting them down in some corner to hatch. The Praying Mantis prepares a very elaborate nest for her eggs, made out of two materials, a soft spongy matter for the inside and a gummy varnish outside; it contains a large number of eggs, and we shall study exactly how the nest is made in a later chapter. One family of beetles, the Tortoise Beetles, makes very similar nests, though of

22

EGG-CASE OF COCKROACH
Hugh Main

EGG-CASE OF PRAYING MANTIS
Hugh Main

much smaller size; some are shaped like tiny boats or cradles.

Where a whole colony of insects live together, such as ants,

bees, or wasps, the larvæ are looked after by special attendants, for they are extraordinarily helpless little creatures
and cannot do anything for themselves ; but the eggs which
produce larvæ of an independent nature, such as caterpillars,

EGG-CASE OF THE INDIAN GOLDEN TORTOISE
BEETLE ON THE UNDER-SIDE OF A LEAF

with nobody to look after them, must be suitably placed so
that they can shift for themselves, for most of these little
things are very delicate, and if they were obliged to wander
about to find food when they first emerged many of them
would be liable to die of starvation. But wherever insects'
eggs are laid we may be quite sure that they are not placed
there by chance ; it is because that is the best place for
them, and the little larvæ will be within reach of everything

they require directly they hatch out. When an insect first emerges from the egg it is called a larva, or grub, or caterpillar.

The larva of the stick insect may be watched creeping out of its egg, and it is a delightful sight, for the manner in which its limbs are packed into the shell is amazing. The legs are

CATERPILLAR OF THE TAU MOTH CREEPING FROM THE EGG WITH ITS SPINES TELESCOPED

THE SAME CATERPILLAR AN HOUR LATER

folded and the body rolled up, and there is no space to spare anywhere. Of course it is very small when it hatches, but when one compares it with the egg it came out of it seems quite impossible that the shell could ever have held it.

Some little caterpillars are armed with spines when they first emerge, and these would take up more extra room than the egg allows. The caterpillar of the Tau Silk Moth, which is found in South Europe, is one of these. This caterpillar has long, branched spines, but at the moment it pushes itself out of the egg these have the appearance of little buds, and they expand to their full length an hour later. Each spine

25

is divided into a certain number of sections, and as each section is neatly telescoped into the next below it the whole spine is contained inside the bottom section ; this is the way in which room is economized inside the eggshell. When the spines expand they are pushed up joint by joint exactly like a telescope.

As larvæ grow they change their skin at intervals, and at each change of skin (or moult) the old skin splits and the larva frees itself, clothed in a new and larger skin. As a general rule the number of times this happens is five, but insects may become mature with three moults, as the house fly, or they may have as many as thirty moults, as the seventeen-year cicada of America.

The larva is not only getting a larger body at each moult, but great changes in its structure are also being gradually brought about, and as it nears the perfect form these changes become more noticeable. For instance, winged grasshoppers show at the third moult tiny leaf-like lobes which are the first appearance of wings. At the next moult these are larger, and at the last the perfect wings appear. It must not be imagined that because they appear suddenly or in an altered form

when the old skin is cast their growth has therefore been sudden. All development is very slow, and these wings and other organs develop little by little under the skin, so that when the outer skin splits they appear ready formed.

YOUNG GRASSHOPPER WITH WING-LOBES

Insects have a hard outer skin which is really made up of several layers tightly pressed together ; between them is a substance called chitin (which means tunic) which forms a tough suit of armour all over the insect to prevent injury to its wonderful, delicate organs. The outer skin is more or less thick according to the group the insect belongs to and the kind of life it leads. It is hardest in beetles, many of which seem to be clothed in plated metal, their layers of chitin being still further strengthened by tiny supporting pillars of chitin, so that they can stand a tremendous amount of pressure without injury. In all growing insects this tunic is tough, but not hard and stiff as in the adult.

It is in the next layer underneath the chitin that growth is carried on. All skin is made up of cells, and the outer layer of cells of this skin under the chitin increases steadily in number, so that instead of being stretched flat the skin lies in folds packed into the outer covering. When the tunic is packed so tightly that it cannot hold any more the larva stops feeding and rests; and while it rests a fluid forms below the outer skin and pushes it off so that it splits, and the folds of the new skin underneath, having nothing now to keep them back, spread out and straighten and harden like the old skin. The insect larva seems to be growing in some miraculous fashion, but it is really this expansion of the crumpled skin which is taking place; and the crumpled skin is due to the multiplying of minute cells, so that the growth has in reality been very gradual.

This is what is happening when your caterpillar or silk-worm stops feeding, looks sick, and then sheds its skin. And when you realize that it even sheds the skin of its digestive tube and its air-tubes at these times you will understand why it looks so sick, and why caterpillars so often die either just before or during a moult.

By far the greater part of an insect's life is taken up in growing and developing, and when once the perfect form is reached the insect does not grow any more. The time of development varies very much in the different groups of insects. Some flies can go through their development in twelve days, while an American cicada takes seventeen years to develop!

There are many young insects which are entirely different in appearance and in habit from their parents, and all these have to go through a certain rest-period as pupæ, when they remain still, with all their activities suspended—usually in a hard envelope of chitin to protect them from enemies—while the important changes in their structure, both outward and inward, are taking place.

What can be more different in appearance than a caterpillar and a butterfly, for instance ? The caterpillar with its long body, several pairs of short, stout walking legs, and claspers, no wings, and a mouth formed for cutting up bits of the leaves on which it feeds ; the butterfly with slender body, six long, slim legs, mouth formed into a long sucking-tube, and two pairs of wings covered in coloured scales. One can scarcely think of these as the same creature, and yet one has developed from the other, and this stupendous change has been brought about gradually in the moults of the caterpillar by the old cells of the old growth drying up and new cells forming new growths folded under the outer skin. We understand why a caterpillar needs a definite rest-period in which to develop into such a new creature.

We are so accustomed to the idea of a caterpillar turning into a butterfly that we hardly give a thought to the wonder of it ; but it is not a simple fact for the uneducated mind to grasp. The Indian farmer sees his fields full of caterpillars, and prays to his gods to remove the pest. He is quite content that his prayers are answered when he sees the number

CATERPILLAR OF PAINTED LADY CHANGING
INTO A CHRYSALIS
O. J. Wilkinson

of caterpillars growing less and less, until finally there is not one to be seen. What has happened is, of course, that they have gone under the soil to pupate, but when they come out again with wings the Indian does not recognize them as the same insect. He only knows that the caterpillars which were devouring his crops have entirely disappeared, and he does not think of destroying these winged insects which do him no harm : he does not realize that they may be the

29

means of bringing other little caterpillars into the world to destroy his crops again. How should he recognize two insects which have no character in common as being the same?

CATERPILLAR PUPA AND BUTTERFLY OF SMALL
CABBAGE BUTTERFLY
Hugh Main

Insects which are so different in the larval stage must rest while the final transformation is being carried out. Such insects are the sawflies, flies, beetles, etc. None of these when they are young bear any resemblance to their parents, and they all have a definite rest-period. But in some orders there is not this marked difference between the larvæ and the mature insects; they are sufficiently alike to be recognized as belonging to one another. A young grasshopper

30

SAWFLY GRUBS

LEAF INSECT JUST HATCHED

Hugh Main

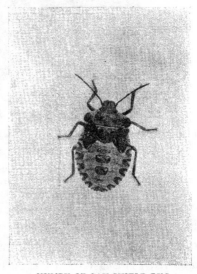

NYMPH OF OAK SHIELD BUG

Hugh Main

31

would never be taken for anything else. Neither would a young stick insect or a young beaked insect, or many others which are very like the parents—except that they are, of

POPLAR HAWK MOTH AND EGGS
H. Shirley

course, smaller. There is no resting period for this type of insect; in the last stages—which can be recognized by certain characters—they are called nymphs instead of larvæ, and with the last moult they become mature.

When the period of development is over all the most

32

important events of the insect's life are crammed into the short time which remains to it. Comparatively few insects live long in the perfect state. Pairing is begun at once, and many and wonderful are the schemes by which insects find their mates with as little waste of time as possible. When pairing is over the male soon dies; he has done his duty toward the next generation, and nature does not require him any longer. The female then devotes all her energies to placing her eggs in the place most suitable to the needs of the new brood; when she has accomplished this she will not live long either; she has done all she can for her family, and there is no need for her to go on living.

CHAPTER II

WHY INSECTS VARY

HAS it ever occurred to you to wonder why there should be such an extraordinary number of species of insects and why there should be such an immense variety of forms among them?

We see the soft-bodied butterflies which squash if we do not hold them very carefully; they have a trunk for sucking fluids and large wings for carrying them about in the air where they spend most of their time. Then we see the glossy hard-coated beetles which live in rotten tree-logs, whose armoured bodies we should find very difficult to injure even if we wished to do such a thing, and whose mouth-parts are a strong pair of jaws with jagged edges for cutting off pieces of the wood on which they feed. Think of the ant, with its brisk little legs and slender waist; then think of the bumble-bee, with its furry body and no kind of a waist at all. Think of the different lives led by ants and butterflies. And yet these are all insects.

There is no such variety of form among the other groups of animals. Take birds, for instance; of course there are large birds and small birds, and birds of every shade of colour, and there are certain varieties of form among them, but the general structure of their body and limbs and organs

SOFT-BODIED BUTTERFLY (CAMBERWELL BEAUTY)
H. Shirley

BRITISH DOR BEETLES WITH
HORNY BODIES

A HORNY TROPICAL BEETLE
THAT LIVES IN WOOD

35

is the same. And at least all birds have feathers and at least they all have beaks.

THE FURRY BUMBLE-BEE

But among insects not even the mouth has the same form. Some have a pair of jaws; some have a beak; and some (such as gnats) have what may be best described as a sucking spear. Some have sucking trunks (as butterflies and moths); some have licking tongues (as flies and bees); and a few have no mouth at all!

Their legs too show a great difference in shape according to the use the insect makes of them. Many of the beetles which live in soil or rotten wood have the front pair broadened toward the tip for scooping out their burrows. The Mole Cricket can beat them all at digging; he has a powerful pair of flat spades instead of front feet, and it is a wonderful sight to see him dig himself in. A few swift

WATER-BEETLE, FIRST, SECOND, AND THIRD LEGS
Hugh Main

strokes with his shovels, and he has vanished, leaving only a movement of the soil which is being pushed out of his passages. There is a curious slim brown insect which is

MOLE CRICKET
Hugh Main

SMALL STAG BEETLE IN BURROW IN WOOD
Hugh Main

found in ponds, the Long Water Scorpion, with a long siphon for breathing at the end of its body. This insect has

37

developed its front pair of legs into instruments for catching its prey—any of the small creatures which are found in

THE LONG WATER SCORPION

water. The tips of the legs are sickle-shaped, with a strong joint, and the forearm has a groove into which the sickle fits like the blade of a penknife. When anything swims

38

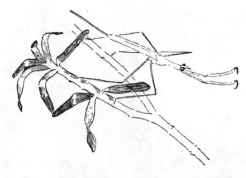

LONG WATER SCORPION WAITING FOR PREY

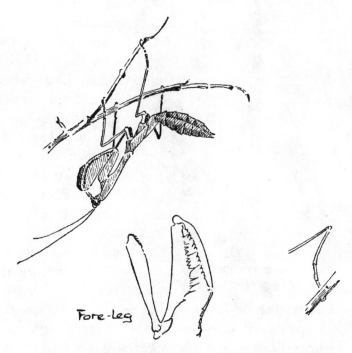

Fore-leg

A YOUNG PRAYING MANTIS WHICH HAS HIND-LEGS FOR GRIPPING,
AND FORE-LEGS FOR TRAPPING ITS PREY

39

within reach the scorpion shoots out its forearm, and the clasp closes down into the groove and holds the little

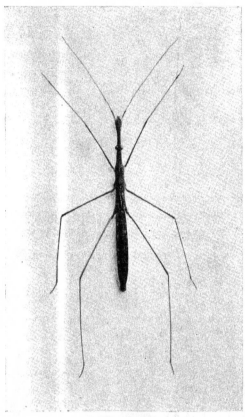

POND SKATER

Hugh Main

creature fast. The Praying Mantis too has a very useful pair of front legs for the same purpose. The inner surface of the last two joints have strong spines which close on one another like the teeth of a trap, and hold the struggling victim in a vicious grip from which there is no escape.

Some legs, as those of the grass-hopper tribe, are very long for jumping, and in other insects which only need their legs to cling with they are very short. In water insects such as Boatmen and the water-beetles the hind-legs are turned into oars, and are fringed with long hairs to help them to put up more resistance against the water as they propel themselves through it; while those

40

that skate about on the surface, such as the Pond Skaters, have their legs and bodies covered with fine short hairs growing thickly like velvet, which prevent them from being wetted; they are so light that they only bend the water film, their feet making

GRASSHOPPER

dimples in it as they skim along the top. The dimples are sufficiently deep to make shadows on the bottom of a shallow pool on a sunny day, but the water film will not break and let the insect through because of the particular form of its feet. We could go on for a very long time finding points on which insects vary from one another, but it is not so easy to discover points of resemblance—characters in which they are alike.

What, then, are the rules for distinguishing insects from the various other little creatures with which we might confuse them? For all these we have just mentioned are insects, although they differ so much in form.

The most important points to remember are that an insect has six legs (the perfect insect—this rule does not apply to larvæ) and that it has a jointed body. First comes the head, then the fore-part of the body, to which the legs are attached —usually this fore-part appears to be in one piece, but it really has three joints—and lastly comes the hinder part of the body, which is also jointed, although the joints are often not noticeable. If we remember this very simple description we shall not go very far wrong when examining some puzzling

41

forms. Mites when they are young also have six legs, but we know them from insects because their bodies are all in one piece instead of being jointed. Woodlice and millipeds and centipeds have jointed bodies, but they have more than

WOODLICE, TOP AND UNDER-SIDE
Hugh Main

six legs, which are attached to all segments of the body instead of to the fore-part alone as in insects.

Now the reason why there are such countless different types of insects is because this body of theirs is able to take different forms. It is rather like a kaleidoscope, a toy which used to be such a favourite and could be bought at any toy-shop. It consisted of a cylinder containing a lot of little bits of coloured glass at one end ; as the cylinder turned it made new patterns by shaking the bits of glass into different positions—and yet they were always the same pieces. So with insects ; out of the same elements thousands of different forms of insects appeared with different organs, different habits, and sometimes of totally different appearance.

Yet all these varieties of beautiful and wonderful forms must have developed from one type of insect. Probably it was a long-bodied insect, this ancient type, rather like an earwig, and of an uninteresting appearance. But these ancient insects had the power of changing the form of their body if it was necessary; and when these changes were inherited their descendants differed more and more from the old type, until we come down to the endless multitude of forms which exists to-day.

MILLIPED
Hugh Main

It was long, long years ago, at the time when plants first learnt to bear blossoms, that insects began to appear in profusion and in many varieties of form. We find traces of gigantic dragonflies, wasps, flies, and cockroaches, etc., in fossil form; that is to say, only fragments are found, for the greater part of the body has usually crumbled away.

In those remote ages it was comfortably warm on the earth, and all vegetation grew luxuriantly, as it does to-day in the tropics. There were not so many species of animals in any of the groups which exist to-day, so there was plenty of food for all, and none had much trouble in finding it. But after that came an Ice Age, and all the creatures which could not adapt themselves to the new climate died off or had to remain

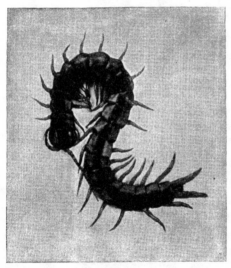

CENTIPED

Hugh Main

in the warmest parts of the earth, which, of course, became rather crowded.

Then it was that the insects had their chance. You will understand what an immense advantage it was, when the ordinary conditions of life altered, to have the power to change their form and food and habits and to develop new species, some of which were bound to fit in with the new conditions. This is what was done by all the plants and creatures which survived those times ; if they had not had this power of forming new species they would all have died out, as some of the old types of plants and giant animals and reptiles died out ; instead of this we know that insects existed in quite remote ages, and they still exist to-day in every corner of the globe which offers the chance of a living, however scanty. And because in those perpetual struggles with new surroundings only the strongest species survived,

44

whenever the little insect appears in some new corner where it has not been found before it has probably come to stay.

It is this power of adapting itself to some change in its surrounding conditions which is the secret of its success. Very often it is man who makes this change in its conditions. When our colonists open up a new piece of country, cut down trees, and clear the ground for their crops they are bound to be taking away the food of countless millions of insects and other creatures. And the numbers of these will have to grow less for lack of food. What will the little insects do ? You may be quite certain that in such a case they will— some of them, at least—adapt themselves to new food, and they may take to these new plants which the colonists are growing for their own use—corn, fruit, or vegetables. And, if this plant suits them, they will probably multiply very fast through having such abundance of food to hand, and man will have to use very drastic measures to prevent his crops from being cleared off altogether. This is what occurs when an insect which has perhaps been hardly noticed before suddenly becomes a pest by increasing in great numbers. Yet man has only himself to blame in the matter, for it is he who has upset the balance of nature. If he can wait long enough there will probably come on the scene some other insects which prey upon the one which is destroying his crops ; and as the pest increases it will provide an increase of food for the insects which prey upon it, until they bring down its numbers to normal again ; thus the balance of nature will be restored and adjusted to the new conditions which man has brought about. But man cannot afford to wait for the pest to be regulated by these natural means. His new crops are also struggling with new conditions, for plants too have to adapt themselves, and while they are improving themselves to cope with new dangers man has to protect them against pests by using the best means in his power. And even when the plants are established they will still be liable to be used as food for quantities of insects, because nature keeps the balance only by allowing them to prey upon one another so that there may be food enough for all. If man will insist upon growing an extra lot of plants all in one place he must be prepared to fight for them against very tiny foes who, in spite of their minute size, are capable of resisting attack in many unexpected ways. This is the reason why we have to spend such enormous sums of money every year on keeping down insect pests. Insects have found in man an unlimited food producer, because he collects and stores for his own use larger quantities of materials than any other living creature.

Think of the different foods insects live upon ; and we must remember at the same time that their bodies are specially formed for their food. They will have particular mouths for eating it, and probably other parts of their bodies, their limbs or their internal organs, will be adapted for collecting it or discovering it. All new conditions mean that new habits must be formed to cope with them, and new habits must be supported by new organs. This is the bargain which nature makes with all creatures which change their manner of living for one for which they have not been formed. And nature is very exacting ; the penalty for not fulfilling their part of the bargain is death to that species. But insects are able to fulfil their part because of their wonderful power of varying.

46

These are some of the foods of insects : rotten wood, growing wood, bark, leaves, flowers, fruit, seeds, pollen, honey, fur, hairs, feathers (one tiny insect related to the wasps actually lives inside the quills of feathers !), coffee, tobacco, and various dried goods (one beetle even gets its living off Cayenne pepper !), corn, flour, sugar, cheese, bacon, paper, meat, cloth. And carnivorous insects live on other insects—snails, worms, etc. This is how some insects have managed to get a living in a world where everybody has a great struggle to fit in.

Another point on which insects have scored a distinct success is in changing their climate. Anybody who has visited tropical countries knows what a multitude of different kinds of insects are found there compared with cooler parts of the globe. These hot countries are the true homes of insects ; the largest forms, the brightest colouring, the greatest variety are found there ; but they are not so bound to a hot climate that they cannot live in cooler countries. One species may adapt itself so that it can live nearly anywhere. Some species have an extraordinary range. For instance, the Clouded Yellow is found from the Arctic zone to the tropics, and in four out of the five continents. The form which represents it in the fifth continent (Australia) is so like it that it could easily be mistaken for the same species.

The Painted Lady is another world-wide form, with a closely related species in Australia ; it has been called the Desert Butterfly because of its having penetrated into particularly dry regions where no other butterflies are seen.

An excellent example of this power of adapting themselves to change of climate came before us quite lately. The

47

THE PAINTED LADY
Hugh Main

Praying Mantis has always been considered a tropical insect. By far the greater number of species are found in the hot

belts, and only a few in temperate zones.   Yet the expedition
to Mount Everest came across mantises at a height of 16,500

PRAYING MANTIS

feet ! This fact proves that it is possible for at least some
members of the group to adapt themselves to a very cold
climate, and there must also have been other insects in their
neighbourhood upon which they could feed.

D

In fact, there seem few difficulties in life too great for insects to overcome in one way or another—usually in several ways, so that one at least is almost bound to be successful.

Does their food suddenly fail ? Then they will take to a different food. Have they no organs specially fitted for this new food ? Then they will speedily alter the structure of their organs to meet this requirement. Is the temperature unsuitable to their manner of living ? Then they will alter their manner of living to suit the change of temperature.

So we see that insects are not only efficient and equipped for all the daily needs of their ordinary existence, but they *can even alter their structure and their habits* to become efficient in some quite new state of existence ; and this is the reason why there are such multitudes of forms in every quarter of the globe and in odd nooks and crannies where only an insect could find a living.

CHAPTER III

THE MEANING OF COLOUR

THE shape of an insect and its colours and tones and pattern have a very important value in its life, for nearly all insects depend for their very existence upon being able to vanish into their surroundings whenever they wish to.

Not only is this necessary for insects which are preyed upon and wish to hide from their enemies, but it is quite as necessary for those which prey upon others not to attract the attention of their victims. We must not forget that these predatory insects also have enemies, so it is of double importance to them to be able to disappear.

There are, however, some insects which, on the contrary, seem anxious to attract attention. These wear most striking patterns and gaudy colouring to make themselves as conspicuous as possible; but there is a different meaning in the pattern of these insects, which we will consider presently.

Vanishing is carried out very thoroughly, and the insect's disguises are perfect to the smallest detail—indeed, insects are very thorough in all their little ways. Vanishing is accomplished by them in two ways. Firstly by being of the same colour as the objects among which they are usually found, such as leaves, stones, mossy stems, soil, etc. Secondly by boldly imitating in form and colour one of these objects of their surroundings : and as these particular objects are always those which are not likely to interest their enemies which are out hunting for prey, as long as these insect-mimics do not betray themselves by moving, they will probably escape observation.

KENTISH GLORY MOTH, WHICH IS PROTEC-TIVELY COLOURED IN DIFFERENT SHADES OF BROWN

We can understand why we experience such difficulty in finding mimetic insects when we hunt for them. The mimicry has to be perfect, for such insects are subjected to the scrutiny of art-critics who inspect them at a much closer range of vision than ours, and would be attracted by any glaring fault in the disguise. Besides, these art-critics are hungry, so their search will be much more thorough than our casual hunt for specimens, for hunger makes eyes very keen.

Any mistake in such mimicry may cost these insects their lives, and possibly did cost the lives of many of the first who attempted it ; this would lead to the dying out of the less successful ones, and account for the marvellous exactness of the examples of protective mimicry among insects of to-day.

WOOD TIGER MOTH WITH CONSPICUOUS PATTERN

H. Shirley

It is such a vital necessity to insects to be able to escape notice that only those which have developed a special weapon of defence can afford to dispense with some sort of colour scheme ; otherwise they would probably not survive a single day.

It is almost impossible to realize the great multitude of dangers which visit an insect from the moment that the egg containing it is laid until it has completed its life-cycle. If a young insect could only be warned of the numbers of risks it would run it might think life was not worth living under these conditions, with such very poor prospects of making any success of it, except to supply somebody with a meal.

Suppose we imagine ourselves on a hot, sunny day in summer, when insects are most active, seated on the bank of a lane, or in a wood or meadow or garden, just to watch

53

some of the common, everyday happenings going on all round us and gather a slight idea of the unceasing activities of insects' enemies.

PRIVET HAWK MOTH WITH PATTERNS LIKE BARK
ON ITS WINGS
H. Shirley

First, there are insectivorous birds quartering the ground between them hour by hour ; then there are nuthatches, woodpeckers, and tits on the tree-trunks and branches, investigating every crevice of the bark for insects ; the bushes

54

are full of warblers, linnets, and wrens, looking for the wherewithal to fill their own beaks and the still tinier ones of a nestful of babies. In the fields and meadows are rooks

SCARCE SWALLOWTAIL SUNNING ITSELF
H. Shirley

and starlings stabbing the surface of the ground for insects with tireless energy.

Climbing about among the herbage are parasitic wasps—beautiful, finely organized creatures, with all their senses keenly developed ; their elegant forms, with delicate, quivering antennæ, seem to be exploring every leaf and every blade of grass. There are thousands of species, and almost every group of insects is preyed upon by them. The females are on the watch for grubs, in order to deposit eggs in their helpless backs ; when the eggs hatch out into little

55

parasitic grubs these live on the host until they have done with him—and by that time there is not enough left of him to boast about.

SWALLOWTAIL SUNNING ITSELF
H. Shirley

Under the stones and fallen logs lurk carnivorous beetles, with huge jaws which seem out of all proportion to the head. Active and alert, they can even detect the soft pattering of a caterpillar's little feet passing their den, and few insects go by unharmed.

UNDER THE STONES LURK CARNIVOROUS BEETLES

SCARCE SWALLOWTAIL
H. Shirley

57

Insects in the low herbage fall victims to lizards, toads, snakes, and other creatures.

Winged insects, though they have a better chance, are not free from enemies, for there are swallows and their tribe to chase them in the air ; then there are dragonflies, and also the bold bad assassin flies, those highwaymen of the insect world, which sit about on the foliage on the watch to murder innocent passers-by. Armed with terrible stilettos, these flies drop upon insects from above, fixing them through the body ; and they can attack species much bigger than themselves.

Under the ground their grubs are preyed upon by other grubs and by centipeds and beetles. Even those grubs of gnats and midges which live in tree-holes that collect just sufficient rain-water to make a miniature pool for them are not safe, for they are preyed upon by grubs of flies which hatch out of eggs laid in the same water !

In the egg stage insects are not safe, for they are attacked by chalcids—minute parasitic wasps which can creep into any hole and squeeze through any crack in search of eggs on which to deposit their own. They are the keenest hunters imaginable, for they are never tired, and to see a little mother chalcid setting out on an egg-hunt is a sight never to be forgotten.

These are some of the insects' enemies, but the list does not by any means include all the creatures which depend upon them for food. And when we take into consideration the fact that those enemies we recognize must be only a small fraction of those about which we know nothing, we can only be filled with amazement that any insect survives at all.

And now supposing we are very observant, and are gifted with a fair amount of Sherlock Holmes' intelligence for following up clues—especially if we watch in the fresh hours of the morning or late afternoon—we shall see other sights very marvellous which will give us some insight into the manner in which a number of insects manage to outwit their foes.

CATERPILLAR OF THE CANARY-SHOULDERED THORN MOTH
Hugh Main

In the thorn-bush at our elbow some of the stout knobby twigs slowly come to life, and loop along the branches toward the green leaves; these are the caterpillars of the Thorn Moths, but to see one fixed to the branch by its hind-suckers and thrusting itself out at an angle, held by a silken thread, to look like a growing twig nobody would imagine that it was a little caterpillar with head and eyes and legs complete. Overhead in the buckthorn tree wherever two leaves lie flat upon each other a little shadow may be seen stealthily moving between them and feeding upon the leaf which forms its ceiling; this is the young caterpillar of the Brimstone Butterfly, which takes its siesta during the hot part of the day, shut up, like an oyster in its shell, between two leaves which it has lightly bound together with its own silk.

A piece of lichen-covered bark on an oak spreads a pair of

59

wings and flutters away into the wood—that was the grey and green moth beautifully named Merveille du Jour. One piece of the lichen sits up on end and eats another piece—this is the caterpillar of the Brussels Lace Moth.

The longer we continue to look about with eyes which can pierce their disguises the longer will our list of mimics grow, and we shall discover that most insects bear a resemblance to some part of their surroundings. We can fully understand what has driven them to adopt such cunning schemes of colour : it is the number of sharp-eyed enemies continually hunting them out ; without this protective coloration no insect can escape—unless it has developed some other equally successful weapon of defence.

More marvellous still than those insects which take the colour and tone of their surroundings to escape the notice of creatures which have evil intentions toward them are the insects which mimic some actual object. Some—as we have seen—imitate twigs ; others leaves, sticks, moss, or flowers. In each case of mimicry we shall find that the object which the insect has imitated is just what its natural enemies are not interested in, so that it is not likely to attract their eye. For example, the leaf insect, so long as it remains still among the foliage, is safe, because the birds, monkeys, squirrels, and lizards which prey upon it do not eat leaves. In the case of insects that prey upon others, on the contrary, they of course imitate something which *is* likely to attract insects.

The best-known cases of mimicry are leaf insects, stick insects, twig caterpillars, leaf butterflies and moths, and the Praying Mantis, which imitates blossoms.

Stick insects are long and slender, and can fold their legs

up tightly against the body so that they look exactly like a
piece of stick.   Their front pair of legs has a particular curve

LEAF INSECT AMONG FOLIAGE

at the base so that they can hold them horizontally, fitting
over the head in a straight line : and the body is pale at the
tip, like the broken end of a stick.   The usual colour is
brown or green; if they carry any bright colour it is on
the wings, where it will be invisible to enemies so long as

61

the stick insect remains among the foliage, and is useful in startling a pursuing enemy if suddenly shown in flight.

EUROPEAN STICK INSECT BACILLUS
Hugh Main

Some stick insects have thorny, spiky, or knobby processes, and these are all a great help in their disguise, and make them more difficult to find.

There is one species found in South Europe, and often bred in this country because it is easy to keep in captivity, but it will not survive the winter out of doors.   Another

STICK INSECT
Hugh Main

species, very like it in appearance, which is also bred in England, comes from India : the chief difference between the two species is that a European stick insect has short antennæ while the Indian species has quite long ones.

63

Individuals of both these species differ very much from one another, their colouring being of all shades from a deep purplish brown to a yellow-green. This variation of colour has also a meaning and a value. These insects hatch out in large families, and they feed together on the same bushes ; supposing an enemy were to discover that one of these insects was good to eat, he would still be liable to pass over many more stick insects in searching for the colour which he had just fixed in his eye as suggesting a meal.

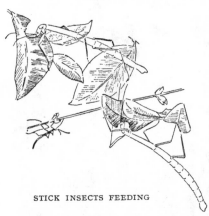

STICK INSECTS FEEDING

The leaf insect is very beautiful and wonderful, and the likeness to a leaf is carried out to perfection. It is just a leaf with legs, and is known as the walking leaf. Those which are most generally reared over here come from South India. The eggs of this particular species are very like little dry seeds. When the little leaf insects are first hatched they are of a reddish colour, just the colour of the buds of some trees. As soon as they begin to feed this changes to green, and on the body the imitation is further carried out by markings like the veins of a leaf. The male, when he is mature, has transparent wings which he uses freely, for he is quite active, and usually found at the top of trees. The female has wings too, but does not use them ; they are marked with leaflike veins to match her body, and the inner edge of each wing

64

has a dark line, so that when they are folded together they look like the midrib of another leaf. To make the decep-

FEMALE LEAF INSECT
Hugh Main

tion quite perfect, as she gets older rust-coloured spots and markings appear exactly as they do in a leaf which is beginning to decay !

E

There are big tropical grasshoppers too with veins and leaf-markings on their large green wings, and we have a record of how one of these deceived some Army Ants, which is one of the best proofs of their being first-class mimics, because Army Ants spend their time in hunting live insects, and one would imagine they were up to any trick. They go out on hunting expeditions in vast hordes, covering the ground and driving insects and small animals and reptiles

out of their hiding-places and overpowering them by their numbers. A naturalist who was observing one of these expeditions in Guiana saw a leaf grasshopper standing quite still in the middle of the ants, while they crawled all over and round it, and never dis-

LEAF GRASSHOPPER

covered that it was an insect and not a leaf! He was so impressed with this sight that when the ants had passed on he picked up the grasshopper and dropped it down in the middle of them again. But the grasshopper held itself quite rigid and made no movement to betray that it was alive, and for the second time the ants passed over it without finding it out. That was the most remarkable test to which any insect-mimic could be put, and is a good proof of the excellence of the disguise.

The beautiful leaf butterflies are familiar to many. The under-sides of the wings represent a dead leaf, the midrib of which is set at an angle, so that when the butterfly rests the wings have the appearance of dead leaves drooping from the stem on which the insect is poised. If the line representing the midrib had been straight up the wing, it would have appeared to spring from the stem at a very unnatural angle for a withered leaf. You see how thorough insects are in the smallest details of their disguises! The inner side of the wings are bright colours, because they only show when the butterfly is flying about and better able to escape from enemies than when it is resting.

Among British insects we find very many examples of mimicry too well known to describe. Everybody knows the twig caterpillars, and how difficult it is to find them when they have folded their three pairs of legs over the fore-part of the body and taken their famous twig attitude.

LAPPET MOTH
Hugh Main

We have lovely examples of leaf-mimicry among British moths large and small, such as the Lappet Moth, and the charming little Thorn Moths, some of which appear early in the year, and imitate in colours and in form the crumpled dead leaves which are still seen hanging on the branches of trees.

A very curious instance of an insect adopting a disguise to lure its prey is that of a Praying Mantis which is found only in the tropics. Three species are known which imitate bright tinted blossoms and feed on the insects that are deceived by

67

the mimicry and come to settle on this sham flower.   Parts of
the mantis's body are expanded into thin plates which are
brightly coloured, usually on the under-side : when it wants

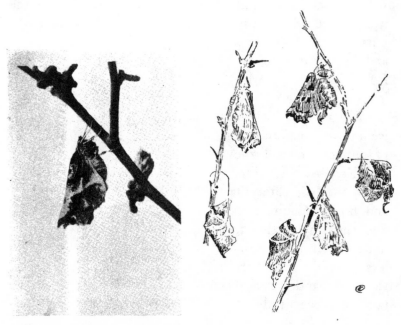

EARLY THORN MOTH HANGING ON
TWIG LIKE DEAD BROWN LEAF
Hugh Main

EARLY THORN MOTHS

to simulate a flower it takes an attitude which exposes these
coloured parts in such a way that they resemble the petals of
a flower, and by sitting among the flowers that it has taken
as a model it attracts insects and devours them.

One which was observed in its natural surroundings had a
lot of small flies settled upon it, evidently allured by the
colours, for they were also on the real flower petals.   The
68

mantis made no attempt to catch these small flies—they were evidently not big enough to trouble about, as they would not make a meal, but she made no movement to frighten them away, for they were useful in making her look more real, and other insects would be attracted. Presently a large fly settled within reach, and at once the false blossom became

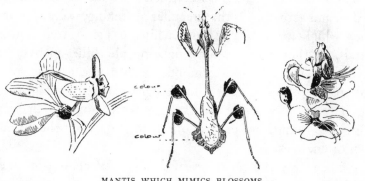

MANTIS WHICH MIMICS BLOSSOMS
Adapted from C. B. Williams

very much alive, and its innocent petals turned into cruel, spined traps which held the fly until it was devoured.

The same mantis was seen searching for a suitable group of flowers on which to take up its position.

Mantises are not quick climbers, being slow and awkward in all their walking movements, and it took this one a long time to reach the tip of a branch which might be expected to bear flowers, but on finding there were only fruit and buds it carefully made its way down again and tried another branch. A second time it was disappointed, because this time there were no flowers at all. It did not remain on the flowerless twigs, but patiently climbed down and sought out

69

a fresh branch. This time it was successful, for a group of flowers was in full bloom, so it settled itself in position turned up its body and showed the coloured under-side, turned out its elbows and its knees and exposed the coloured plates, and lo and behold it was no more an awkward, angular insect, but just a mass of soft pink petals !

There is an Indian species which is coloured in pink or white, and actually has that peculiar glistening, waxy appearance which we notice in pure white or pale-tinted flower petals. Other mantises have dark purple, blue, mauve, or green showing on parts of the body. But in every case it is able to keep these colours out of sight when they might be a danger to it—when, for instance, it is climbing a branch or is on the ground, and bright colours might attract the attention of enemies.

We see now the meaning of this special coloration and special forms among insects. It is the unceasing vigilance of their many enemies which has forced them to adopt these various and wonderful schemes to escape notice, and only those insects which have developed some other means of protection are able to break the rule of making themselves invisible whenever they rest.

CHAPTER IV

HOW INSECTS PROTECT THEMSELVES

ONE of the laws of nature which we are sure to dis-cover for ourselves sooner or later, if we study the daily doings of any group of creatures, is that if a species which has many enemies can withstand their attacks long enough it is certain in the course of time to develop some kind of protection against them. Or perhaps we ought to put it in another way, and say that *unless* a species can evolve some kind of defence against its enemies it will finally be wiped out—as of course has happened to a great many species in the past.

Enough has been said about one protective habit that some insects adopt, namely, the taking on of shapes and colours which make them very difficult to find, and then " laying low and saying nuffin," like Brer Rabbit. These insects are obliged to move about when they want food, but they usually choose the dusk in which to be active, and in the half-light of dawn or evening of course their movements are not so noticeable.

Whether an insect is preyed upon or not, it is more prudent of it to hide itself; and this is such a general rule that the coloration of a specimen very often gives us a clue to what sort of country it lives in. Insects which inhabit dry, parched land and deserts are dull-coloured or blotched, and

71

many are the colour of sand, and so on. But there are also many insects which are just the reverse. Instead of adopting discreet colours and crafty patterns so that they melt

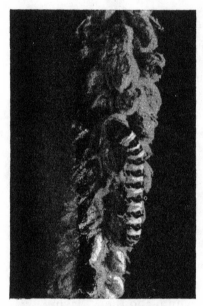

into their background and are with difficulty distinguished from it, these have, on the contrary, very gaudy tints and bold designs, so that they attract attention in a quite reckless fashion among their natural surroundings. This is called warning or defiant or aggressive coloration, and is valuable to the insect that possesses it because it acts as a signal to enemies, warning them that this insect is for some reason undesirable as food. It may be that the insect has developed particular body-juices which give it a

CATERPILLAR OF MULLEIN MOTH WITH
AGGRESSIVE COLORATION

Hugh Main

disagreeable flavour, as the ladybird or some of the brightly marked beak insects and wasps have done. If there is any choice of food their enemies will take anything else rather than touch these insects which warn them off by their bright colours and striking patterns. Now this scheme of coloration is not carried out in thoughtful consideration for their enemies, as some might suppose, to save them from the shock of a disagreeable mouthful, but as a double protection, to

72

ensure these insects getting the full advantage of having a disagreeable flavour or similar protection. The fact of being distasteful would not be sufficient defence in itself if the enemy were obliged to taste the insect first before finding it out. Most insects are very fragile, and by the time the

ORIZABA CATERPILLAR IN AN ATTITUDE WHICH SHOWS ONLY THE
LEAF-GREEN UNDER-SURFACE OF ITS BODY

enemy had satisfied himself that it was not to his taste the insect would be so injured that it would be of small account to it whether its mutilated corpse were eaten or just left for scavengers to clear away. Therefore some sort of warning is necessary to call attention to these insects and notify to anyone concerned that they have a special protection and that it would be unwise to interfere with them. One experiment at trying to eat an insect which carries these warning signals will teach the enemy their meaning, and the rest of that species of insects will benefit; but probably instinct

73

teaches the enemy to avoid the distasteful forms, and unless forced by hunger or goaded by boredom (such as may happen to those kept in captivity) they will not attempt to risk an unpleasant experience.

Some of these warningly coloured insects are especially beautiful. It suggests to us that bright coloration is natural to all insects, and that it is their numerous enemies which force them to adopt dull, neutral tints, such as green, brown, or grey, because those which are fortunate in having special protection ignore the tiresome restriction of plain clothes and deck themselves in the most gorgeous colours they can produce. It is delightful to see these insects showing themselves in the bright sunshine, or feeding fearlessly in the open instead of making special efforts to keep themselves hidden.

Not only those insects which have disagreeable flavours to their body-juices are warningly coloured ; there are others

that are armed with certain glands baldly called stink-glands. These produce some strong-smelling fluid which the insects are able to squirt out suddenly at anything which disturbs them. Some, such as the Puss

CATERPILLAR AND EGG OF PUSS MOTH
Peter Scott

Moth caterpillars and many beetles and beaked insects, eject this fluid from the tail or from their mouths. The Bombardier Beetle sends up what looks like a puff of bluish smoke when it shoots out in defence a jet of acid, which is a most

74

effective weapon against enemies. The acid of the well-known Blister Beetles is strong enough to burn the skin of a human being, and is made use of for raising blisters. These beetles are related to our British Oil Beetles, and if interfered with they put out a fluid from the joints of the legs. To prepare blister-plasters the Blister Beetles have to be killed and dried and crushed to powder, which is then made into a paste.

BLISTER BEETLE

Hugh Main

Many species of ants can eject a stream of formic acid from their mouths, and this weapon is especially useful to them if the nest be attacked. The soldier-ants will take an attitude with the body bent underneath them and the head pointed skyward, and throw up the poison fluid as high as five inches.

Some caterpillars put up from their head a pair of flabby horns which leave a few drops of scent upon anything with which they come in contact. The scent from these glands is not always unpleasant to human beings—in many cases, on the contrary, it is quite agreeable. The scent given out by the caterpillars of the Japanese Swallowtail is delicious, being the spicy scent of its food-plant.

What is called a terrifying attitude is also largely used in

75

defence. It is not unusual among our British caterpillars, such as Elephant Hawks, Puss Moths, and Swallowtails; the thorax is usually bunched up to give the impression of a giant head, with two false eyes. The same green caterpillar of the Japanese Swallowtail just referred to looks like some quaint monster when it takes this terrifying attitude, with the real head held down out of sight.

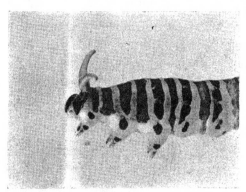

SWALLOWTAIL BUTTERFLY LARVA SHOWING SCENT-ORGANS

Hugh Main

Various other methods of practising frightfulness are employed, such as the swaying of the body to and fro while it is more or less distorted, accompanied sometimes by alarming noises, such as hissing or squeaking.

Other forms of protection are spines and hairs upon the body which hurt the mouth of the

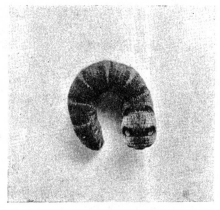

SMALL ELEPHANT HAWK MOTH CATERPILLAR THREATENING

Hugh Main

adversary and prevent him from swallowing his victim.

76

Few birds will touch a hairy caterpillar, and some hairs, being branched, are particularly irritating to the skin, and will even set up a rash on delicate skins.

CATERPILLAR OF LOBSTER MOTH IN TERRIFYING ATTITUDE

Most people know the brilliant little scarlet and white caterpillar of the Brown-tailed Moth, common on our hedges, and have probably suffered—if they attempted to handle them—through the so-called stinging hairs. This term is misleading, as they cannot be said to sting in the same

77

sense as the leaves of stinging nettles, for instance ; there is
no gland attached, nor are the hairs grooved to allow the
passing of any fluid.   It is the branched tips which get into

HAWK MOTH CATERPILLAR RESTING
Hugh Main

the pores of the skin and set up inflammation in some
people.

If we wish for a proof that the aggressive coloration of
these gaudy insects is indeed a very successful scheme to
warn off the majority of their enemies we could not find
anything more convincing than the remarkable fact that

these particular forms are mimicked in colour and pattern by other insects which do not indeed possess these defensive weapons, but are, on the contrary, quite good to eat. These

ELEPHANT HAWK AND JAPANESE SWALLOWTAIL CATERPILLARS

mimics take advantage of the distaste which their enemies have connected with a startling appearance, and with these sham warnings have a better chance of escape.

It may not be clear how one can tell which species is mimicking the other, for it might be argued that those carrying warning colours may be mimicking the edible species. But usually on examining the patterns of the

CATERPILLAR OF LIME   CATERPILLAR OF PRIVET
HAWK MOTH   HAWK MOTH

Peter Scott

two insects it will be seen which is the true pattern or form. For instance, there may be a transparent spot like a little window, so often to be found on coloured wings of butterflies, and this will be represented by a spot of pale colour on the wing of the mimic which gives it the same

79

appearance, but is not a transparency, or the ragged edge of a wing may be mimicked by light and dark tones on a wing

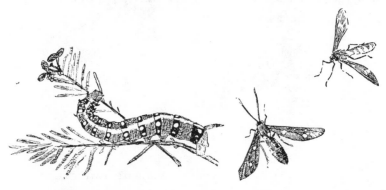

CATERPILLAR OF SPURGE HAWK MOTH
Peter Scott

MOTH WHICH MIMICS A
PARASITIC WASP

which has not that form. Another reason for believing this theory of true and false warnings is that various forms of false warning may be found leading up gradually to a more or less correct imitation of the insect which has reason for carrying warning signals.

HORNET CLEARWING MOTH
Hugh Main

Not only in appearance, but often in habit, the mimicry is carried to a higher degree. The Hornet Clearwing, which has the general coloration of wasps or hornets, moves its wings with an excited buzzing in precisely the same manner as an angry wasp. Until they are examined closely, and especially until the difference in the shape of the antennæ is noted, anybody not familiar with the Hornet Moth might be excused for thinking that it belonged to the wasp group.

Interesting experiments have been made to prove that insects wearing these false warning colours do really deceive their natural enemies. One which was carried out in the Zoological Gardens many years ago is especially striking. There is a large fly called Volucella which in general appearance and colour resembles a bumble-bee. Bumble-bees are avoided by most birds and other insectivorous creatures because of their hairy coat, which is very unpleasant and indigestible; most birds, too, dislike the formic acid which supplies the sting with poison. Any insect which stings makes a good model for mimicry, as it is usually avoided as food.

In the experiment referred to above various kinds of birds at the Zoological Gardens were offered bumble-bees. Some refused to touch them; others, perhaps out of sheer boredom, made an attempt to eat them, but without success. After the birds had found out that bumble-bees are not good to eat the perfectly edible fly Volucella was offered to them, but in every single case they would not attempt to touch it, evidently not wishing to risk another such disagreeable experience as they had just gone through. Only one specimen of Volucella was used, and although between thirty and forty experiments were made this one fly survived them all!

CHAPTER V

THE MEANING OF PATTERN

A LITTLE more time must be devoted to the appearance of insects before we leave this for other subjects, for there are still several important points which are too interesting to be passed over. We have to realize that there is a meaning in every spot and line that makes up the colour-scheme of insects, and though we may be filled with admiration by vivid colours and the various ways by which these are intensified, or softened by cunning half-tones, or made to flash like gems, or disappear altogether, yet unless we can read the language of the colour-patterns we shall lose a great deal of pleasure which that knowledge would bring us.

On the wings of butterflies and moths are certain conspicuous spots which are known as eye-spots; these are usually very round, and are darker in the centre, with a light rim, all of these points helping to make them stand out from the rest of the pattern. It is also rather important to notice those which are always placed near the tip of the wing. It has been proved that these spots have a special value to the insects which possess them, because, being so conspicuous, they detract the attention of birds or lizards when they are making an attack upon them from more important parts of the body, where injury would be fatal. The bird aims at what catches his eye, and the butterfly escapes with its life, although with a torn wing.

These attacks on butterflies are made more frequently than might be supposed, especially in hot countries, where

POLYPHEMUS SILK MOTH RESTING WITH EYE-SPOTS PARTLY HIDDEN

there are, of course, far more butterflies than we ever see in England. When a butterfly is resting for a short time is the opportunity for using the eye-spots, because the insect is on the alert; if an enemy should creep up to it—and lizards especially are dreaded foes, being so much the colour of their surroundings, and slow in approaching, yet swift to strike— the blow will be directed at the part which stands out most distinctly, the tip of the insect's wing where the eye-pattern

83

is, and before the enemy has time to get in a second attack the butterfly is off, for a torn tip to its wing will not prevent it from flying. When the butterfly rests for a long time, however, as they often do in dull or rainy weather, hanging on the stems of plants or among herbage, then the eye-spots would be a direct source of danger to it, for the insect is too

inert to escape quickly if it is attacked. On these occasions, before the butterfly settles itself down to sleep, the upper wings, on which are the tell-tale eye-spots, are drawn down behind the lower wings, and these being usually of some protective colour and pattern which blend very well with the background of its resting-place, the butterfly is practically invisible while it is still.

The theory of this use of eye-spots may sound very fanciful. Indeed, when it was first made known many entomologists doubted whether such an explanation could really be accepted, and some were quite noisy in condemning it as impossible, so special experiments were made which proved to be most interesting. A large number of butterflies with eye-spots on their wings were collected from one district ; these were examined, and it was found that the majority had their wings injured just at the tip ; in some cases the eye-spot pattern was completely torn away. Nearly all of these butterflies were still able to fly in spite of their ragged wings. But there was no direct evidence as to what had caused the

84

injury to the wings, for it might just as well have been the result of flying through bushes or tangled undergrowth. So again experiments were carried out to determine this point, and by comparing wings which had been torn by thorns with those which were sus- pected of being injured through the attack of enemies it was satisfac- torily shown that they must have been nearly captured, and have escaped with their lives, through the enemy striking at the wings.

We can watch this pretty little trick taking place on summer days in our own meadows, or wherever Meadow Brown Butterflies or Gatekeepers or any other of our butterflies which carry eye-spots on the tip of the wing are numer- ous. Watch them on a bright, hot day, when they only settle for a few minutes to take a short rest,

MEADOW BROWN BUTTERFLY
RESTING AND SLEEPING

and you will notice that the eye-pattern is very plainly to be seen ; the insects are very wide awake on such days ; it is difficult to take them even with a net. But on a wet or cloudy day we find quite another state of affairs. The butter- flies are dull and very sleepy ; they hang limply from grass stems or foliage ; and it is quite easy to catch them with the hand they are so inert. And if you notice the position of the wings you will find that the butterfly has taken an attitude that completely hides the conspicuous pattern. It has drawn down the front wings behind the hind pair, so that nothing shows but the soft browns and greys which make up the colour-pattern. The butterfly is scarcely noticeable against the browns and greens of the grasses, and there are no doubt a large number of butterflies and moths and other insects which you will pass by without having the slightest idea that they are there.

SWALLOWTAIL BUTTERFLY
Hugh Main

The tails of Swallowtail Butterflies and Moths are thought to have the same use as eye-spots ; that is, to attract the notice of enemies while they are flying, so that they snatch at the tail and miss the head or body, where the injury would be fatal. These tails are very delicate, and in some species they are quite long, as in the Luna Moths of North America and the day-flying Swallowtail Moths of Madagascar, so that they are liable to be injured in a great many ways. In fact, it is more usual to see them—even those reared in captivity

86

—with part of the appendage missing than to see a perfect specimen ; so that there does not seem sufficient evidence to justify our saying that they are of the same value to an insect as eye-spots appear to be.

A surprising fact which has not been known so very long is that patterns may vary in the different seasons. And of course each pattern has a meaning and a value for the owner in that particular season. British butterflies and moths have two seasons, summer and winter ; but in tropical countries there is not the same division of the year, and a butterfly's year alternates in wet seasons and dry seasons. Sometimes there are only two seasons in the year, or there may be several rainy seasons, and several dry seasons between them. In the wet seasons plants grow ; there is plenty of food for caterpillars and excellent opportunities for rearing broods ; so insects pair freely, and there may be several generations ; as food is plentiful for all there is not such a demand for insects as food as in time of scarcity. During the dry season, on the contrary, there are no facilities for rearing broods, because plants die from drought, and whole tracts are left without a green leaf. Therefore insects do not breed, and there are fewer to be found, because many of them burrow below ground and disappear until the rains come. This makes life still more difficult for the insects which remain active and carry on until life is again made possible for a new generation. Not only is the average of risks greater than it is in a short-lived generation, but also those which remain active are hunted more zealously when insect-life is scarce.

Because the life led by insects during these two seasons is so different, some butterflies have two forms which differ most amazingly in size, in pattern, in colour, and even in habits, from one another. So much do they differ that for a long time they were thought to belong to two different species instead of being merely two forms of the same species. The wet-season form is more striking in pattern and colour ; the under-side of the wings often bears spots, because when the butterflies settle to rest for a short time they have many enemies about and must take precautionary measures. The dry-season form is less daringly coloured, swifter in flight, and flies higher ; its periods of rest being longer, the under-side of the wings shows protective coloration, without any of the bright tints which distinguish the wet-season form. Moreover, the eye-spots which are often present in that form are absent in the dry-season form ; we can now follow out the reason for their absence, and can understand for ourselves that the better these butterflies are able to conceal themselves when they take long rests the more hope they will have of escaping from their very numerous hungry enemies, which are all on the prowl during the dry season.

CHAPTER VI

HOW INSECTS GET THEIR COLOURS

BIRDS and butterflies and flowers have certainly the brightest colours of all nature's productions ; the competition is so keen between these that it would be hard to say which is able to show the most vivid tints.

Colours of insects are mostly due to what are called pigments—that is, particular substances which are found in cells forming a layer under the outer skin. All rays of light contain colours, which do not show unless there is something to split them up, as it were. That is exactly what pigment cells do. They absorb certain of the colours from the rays of light as they fall on them, leaving the rest of the colours—or perhaps only one—to be reflected back into the eye. So that what we are really looking at on a gorgeously coloured insect are the colours which have not been left behind in the pigment cells. Insects with densely chitinous skins do not show much colour, because the light cannot reflect from chitin, but is absorbed.

Pigments of insects have the character of remaining without any change for an immense number of years. This is a great advantage for collectors of insects, for the specimens preserved in cabinets will keep their colour almost for ever with ordinary treatment—that is, if the colour is produced by pigments alone, and not through any other means.

This rule applies to a certain number of colours, but not to all. There is a particular sky-blue which is brilliant while the insect is alive, but begins to change when it is dying, and quite vanishes when it is dead. This being such a very beautiful shade of blue, it is most disappointing that it cannot be preserved. It appears on the wings of some moths and on the body of others ; and there is an Ophion Fly (whose larva preys on the cater-pillars of the large Silk Moths) which has wonder-ful sky-blue eyes, but these too fade directly the insect dies, the colour being pro-bably due to a fluid which dries up when the Ophion dies.

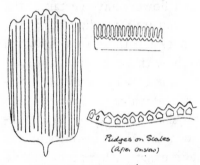

Ridges on Scales
(after Onslow)

SCALE OF BUTTERFLY'S WING

Some of the brightest colours, such as the gorgeous tints on the wings of tropical butterflies, are not due to pigments, and if we study what causes them we make the astounding discovery that they are produced by structures which are them-selves quite colourless. The wings of butterflies and moths and gnats are covered with scales or plumes : tiny flake-like structures, each with a stem which is attached to the surface of the skin, but can be easily brushed off it (which is the reason why a butterfly's wing requires such delicate handling). The scales grow thickly, the base of each row being partly covered by the tips of the next row, so that all overlap a little like tiles on a roof ; indeed they are very like tiles, the stems representing the pegs which keep tiles in

90

place. These scales are of a crystal clearness; there is no trace of any colour in them; so that if we would find a reason for the colours which we admire on those butterflies' wings we must look a little farther and examine the shape and formation of each tiny scale.

It requires a very strong microscope to show this, but we shall discover that each scale, instead of a smooth surface, has a mass of transparent ridges running up it lengthways from the base to the tip. Each ridge is made up of two long, thin plates joined at the top, but slanting away from one another at the bottom, and with air between. It gives us some idea of the size of these tiny ridges when we learn that there are about 1400 ridges to the millimetre on the wing of that wonderful blue butterfly (Morpho), with wings like bright blue satin, which comes from South America. It is much prized by collectors and dealers for its lovely colour, and bits of wings are made up into jewellery and ornaments. There is no fear of the colour fading in these specimens so long as the scales are not injured in any way. They will never change their tint if they remain intact because the colour is not in the wing itself. It is produced by the rays of light glancing in and out of these millions of tiny ridges, set at an exact angle to reflect back the blue only, and the air between the thin films serves to intensify the colour and give it that particular brilliancy. But if after death these delicate ridges should shrink or collapse the shades of colour they produce will naturally alter, and we find that our specimen has faded.

In order to test this theory a piece of glass was specially prepared with fine lines cut in it and set very close together. Of course it was impossible to make ridges constructed like those on a butterfly's wing, for they are far too minute to be copied, but the lines numbered 1900 to the inch, which means that the ridges between them were very tiny. The result was most satisfactory, for it was found that very pure colours were produced in this way, and different colours according to the angle formed by the ridges between the lines. Not only butterflies and moths, but also dragonflies, gnats, and mayflies have these scales for producing colours on their wings : specially formed structures of various designs set at the exact angle which will best break up and reflect the rays of light, and so produce beautiful colours.

The pale green colour which is seen in so many caterpillars, grasshoppers, leaf insects, and others, is due to a quite different cause, for it is produced by the colouring matter which is found in plants—and is, in fact, the same material which colours the plants green. It is called chlorophyll, and is found especially in the stems of growing plants.

Now this green colouring matter is not changed by acids ; therefore the digestive juices, which usually turn food into fluid, have no effect upon it. All this would not be quite so interesting to us if it were not for the fact that chlorophyll is of great value to insects which resemble their surroundings. When an insect feeds upon leaves it takes in chlorophyll, which passes through the digestive tubes and passes out of them again into the body without being altered by the process, still retaining its green colour. This green matter is in the skin of some insects, and matches exactly the leaves which the insect feeds upon.

There is a most interesting proof of how chlorophyll can last for years and years without being changed. The museum at Petrograd possesses in a wonderful state of preservation a mammoth which was found in a bank of frozen mud that had not thawed since the time of its death. In the stomach of this mammoth chlorophyll was found which must have been taken in by the monster with the food which made its last meal. It is supposed that by some accident it fell over into the soft mud of a river-bank and sank into it. The mud froze before the body had time to decay, and so the whole huge beast, with bones and skin complete, was dug out long ages afterward. The rest of the body had undergone a certain amount of change, but the chlorophyll was as green as though it had just been extracted from plants!

As we should naturally expect, the insects with the brightest colours are most active in the daytime. Nocturnal insects are as a rule of dark and sombre colours.

Some of the most gaudy day-flying insects, which look so conspicuous when held in the hand, or put on a dark background, are in reality not conspicuous when they are in brilliant sunshine, and especially among bright coloured flowers. There are some beautiful little bronze beetles always on sunny days to be found sitting in the centre of the yellow hawkweed flowers which grow on chalky downs. When seen quite near this is a very striking little beetle, with its shining wing-cases like polished metal, but eating pollen on a yellow flower in the sunshine it is scarcely noticeable unless one looks for it. So with the Rosechafers, those beautiful copper-red or green-bronze beetles which are also pollen-feeders. They are only abroad in bright sunshine, and are less likely to attract attention among the flowers than a dull-coloured beetle would be.

There is a wonderful example of this shown by the chrysalids of the Peacock, Red Admiral, and Tortoiseshell Butterflies.

Sometimes the colour of the chrysalis may be a bright golden, as if it were made of molten gold. But others are light brown or green. Professor Poulton named the golden chrysalids the " rock-surface variety," and pointed out that whenever these particular caterpillars have the chance of choosing where to hang themselves up before changing into a chrysalis they will pick out a hard, glistening surface, such as a stone. This sort of background exactly suits the colours of the chrysalis ; the light reflected from its surface is not more striking than that from the surface of the stone, more especially if the stone is wet. If, however, the caterpillar has no choice, but feels that his time has come to pupate, and there is no shining surface at hand where instinct tells him there would be little likelihood of the golden colour betraying him, he does the next wisest thing. He

TORTOISE BEETLE, GREEN LIKE THE LEAF IT FEEDS AND RESTS ON
Hugh Main

94

loops together with silk some of the nettle-leaves he is feeding upon to form a little tent, inside which he pupates. It is quite worth the trouble to examine little bunches of nettle-leaves which seem to be netted together, for you will probably be rewarded by finding a chrysalis suspended from the ceiling of some of these little canopies.

But we see metallic coloration in a great many beetles, and it is in this order of insects that we are accustomed to look for examples. Many of the moths have metallic scales forming a pattern on the wings, or the whole wing may glitter and show different colours at different times. This is due to

PUPA OF SMALL TORTOISESHELL BUTTERFLY
Hugh Main

the structure of the scales, which reflect different colours according to the side one views them from.

The metallic colour of some of the beetles is caused by the *structure* of the hard covering which they wear like armour. This is formed, as we discovered in Chapter I, of many layers of very thin sheets pressed together so as to make a tough, horny substance. Where the metallic colours are seen on these particular beetles the first sheets are almost transparent;

95

GOLDEN PUPA OF RED ADMIRAL BUTTERFLY IN TENT OF LEAVES OF NETTLE

The front of the tent has been removed.

Hugh Main

next comes a layer which is thickly dotted with cells of colouring matter (pigment) surrounded by a colourless fluid ; below these again comes a dense layer of chitin. As the rays of light strike the surface of the beetle some rays will pass through the transparent layers, missing the pigment cells, till they reach the dense chitin, which they are unable to pierce, so the white light will be reflected back unchanged, not having encountered anything on the way to split it up. But other rays will strike the pigment cells, and some of the colours will be absorbed ; the rest of the colours are reflected back to the eye together with the white rays, and this gives them a peculiar lustrous quality, like shining metal.

In some of the golden beetles we get a satisfying proof of this fact. The pigment cells absorb the blue, green, and violet rays of a beam of light ; these rays being quenched, only the red, orange, and yellow remain to be reflected, which, together with the white light that pierces the colourless fluid, produce the brilliant warm yellow that we call golden.

Now this colourless fluid is sometimes reduced for a while ; the food the beetle is taking does not produce it in sufficient quantity. Then the wing-cases will change to a dull ochrous red, and the metallic gleam will entirely disappear for a time. When the insect dies it will lose its golden colour altogether, because this colourless fluid dries up, but if the specimen is preserved in something of a greasy nature, such as glycerine, the metallic tint remains.

CHAPTER VII

SENSES OF INSECTS

THE sense of smell is of great importance to the majority of insects, because it brings them knowledge of certain things which play a serious part in their life-history. The organ of smell is like an instrument, set to catch certain smells which are important to them in one way or another, and other smells will not be noticed, because their organ of smell is not attuned to them. It is smell which guides them to their food, sometimes helps them to find their mates, and enables the mother insect to choose a place for her eggs suitable for the larvæ which will hatch out of them.

In many cases this food for the future generation is not what the mother insect feeds upon herself. For instance, some kinds of flies feed upon honey or nectar, but lay their eggs upon putrid matter or garbage. So we find the organ of smell in these insects is attuned, as it were, to two smells ; one stirs up suggestions in her which induce her to eat, the other stirs up suggestions which induce her to lay eggs. Each of these two smells has a different effect upon the insect, for each affects different organs of her system, but other smells which we should consider much stronger than these may not be noticed by her.

Burying Beetles, guided by the sense of smell, will fly a

long distance direct to the spot where some small dead creature is lying, and will not perceive the scent of lilac or roses, which we find so attractive. The reason for this is that a corpse has an important bearing upon the life of Burying Beetles; it forms their food and the food of their larvæ; but roses and lilac hold no interest for them, and therefore their sense-organs are not formed to bring these scents to their notice.

The organ of smell in the majority of insects is in the antennæ. Not all insects have this sense developed to the same extent, because not all need it. Dragonflies rely for all the important matters of their lives upon their enormous protruding eyes. These consist of about 16,000 lenses each, and can spy out tiny gnats and midges, and aid the wings in darting after them with unerring directness. Their food consists of flying insects; their mates put out no scents; their eggs are laid in water; therefore they can arrange all their business without the help of a sense of smell.

The antennæ of dragonflies are small, and as far as we know are of no particular use to them. Those of the larvæ are larger and do evidently possess a sense-organ, but this is probably for testing the purity of the water. A sense of smell is not of the same importance to insects which pass most of their time in water as to those which live on land.

Butterflies have highly developed eyes, but the sense of smell also is necessary to them. They are doubtlessly guided chiefly by sight in finding their food, but they also rely upon smell. If you wish to test this, offer sweetened water to a butterfly upon any colourless object or upon the tip of your finger; it will bend its delicate antennæ to the spot, and

99

having thus perceived the scent of the liquid it will unroll its proboscis and feed. The female butterfly when she is ready to deposit her eggs will flit among a mass of green

SMALL TORTOISESHELL BUTTERFLY SHOWING
COILED TONGUE
Hugh Main

leaves belonging to various plants, select that particular species on which her caterpillars feed, and lay her eggs there. This selection is accomplished by the sense of smell.

Ants, we find, can get through nearly all the events of their lives without the help of sight ; some species, indeed, are quite blind, and others can perceive only movements and

100

the difference between darkness and light. It has been proved by experiment that ants when they have had their

EGGS OF SPECKLED WOOD BUTTERFLY
ON GRASS
Hugh Main

eyes painted over with varnish can still carry out all their duties as comfortably as though they could see. But when the antennæ are injured they cannot carry on any of their usual activities. They are unable to find their way home

101

even if put down near the nest ; they will not feed ; they do not know friend from foe, and if pupæ from their nest are given to them they will take no notice. This last fact is sure evidence that they have not got all their senses, for to normal worker ants the pupæ and larvæ and eggs belong-ing to their colony are the most important objects in existence.

BUTTERFLY LAYING EGG

For all these things ants rely solely upon their sense of smell, and the organ of smell is in the antennæ. The great object in a nest of busy working ants is to waste no time, and to this end there are scent-paths laid for them to follow wher-ever there is greatest traffic, just as good roads are made and kept in good condition around a city. When once the road is made the rest of the workers can race along it at full speed, guided by the scent, so that no time is lost in fulfilling their duties. By their organ of smell they can distinguish the ants of their own colony from those of another. A strange ant will be recognized at once and speedily dealt with, while ants of their own nest can even be separated from the community for some time, and will still be welcomed as friends on their return.

Judging by the behaviour of insects we are quite sure that their organ of *smell* is well developed, but when it comes to the question of *hearing* we cannot be sure to what extent an insect can hear sounds, and some insects are without an

102

organ of hearing as far as we can judge. It is certain that they can feel vibrations, but this is due to quite a different sense-organ. Most insects, and particularly those with very

MOSQUITO, SHOWING HEAD, ANTENNÆ, PALPI, AND
SUCKING SPEAR
Hugh Main

horny skins, have strong hairs and spines in different parts of their bodies ; these hairs pass through the chitin, and are attached to nerves, so that anything which affects them is carried by the nerves to the chief nerve centre, which is the insect's brain. As the insect moves over the ground it knows what the surface is like, and anything approaching it which is heavy enough to cause even a slight vibration will be perceived sooner than by sight. These sensory hairs almost

103

take the place of the organ of hearing ; indeed, some insects require nothing further.   But where there are musical organs

ANTENNÆ, ETC., OF MALE MOSQUITO
Hugh Main

used by insects we should expect some special organ to catch those sounds, for the sensory hairs do not all record vibrations of the air, and if an insect makes a certain sound it is only reasonable to suppose that it is for the purpose of making itself known to other insects of the same species.

104

The hairs on the antennæ will also quiver to certain vibrations. One scientist proved this by fastening a male mosquito to a glass slide and then sounding different notes with a tuning-fork. He found that some caused the hairs to vibrate, and he made the further interesting discovery that these particular notes are the song of the female. When the female is near her song causes the hairs on the male's antennæ to vibrate. If she is to the side of him only the hairs of one antenna will vibrate, and he will move until both are affected, and so will be able to fly straight to her. What need has the mosquito of ears when he has such a delicate organ as this ?

But there is a special organ which in its structure comes far nearer what we call ears. This organ of hearing is on different parts of the body in different insects.

We have now to study insect vision, for we naturally inquire when we see what beautiful forms and colours are produced in the insect world : How much is the insect itself conscious of all this ? Are insects influenced in any way by colour ?

ORGAN OF HEARING IN A GRASSHOPPER'S LEG

There was a time when such an idea was scoffed at. It was considered that " unconscious nature " was created only for human beings to enjoy; also that the creatures which happen to be of use to man are here for that very purpose and no other ; and that those which upset his plans by making use of *him*, and of the things he is trying to preserve, have no reason for their existence, and ought to be wiped off the earth. Some earlier writers took that view, but of late years nature-lovers have not been quite so ready to consider that the whole universe was designed for our welfare and pleasure. Some writers have even considered events from the point of view of the animal they were studying; and that is the only way really to get at the truth. We know quite well that anybody who wants to write a truthful biography will naturally try to put himself in the place of the person he is writing about, and the same rule should apply as far as possible to any life which is described, whether of some distinguished personage or some species of insect. And on careful consideration we shall discover that most of the beauty of plant-life at least was not developed for us at all—although perhaps only human beings can fully appreciate it—but to awaken response in the sense-organs of insects, chiefly those of the higher orders.

Insects vary a great deal in the matter of vision. Some have very good sight; others can see only when they are close to objects; some can just see the difference between light and dark; and some which live habitually in the dark are blind.

Many insects rely upon other organs for getting what they want, and these find a simple type of eye quite good enough for them. The structure of eyes varies enormously, ranging from simple eyes of one lens up to compound eyes, which may be made up of several thousand lenses.

Some insects possess in addition to these wonderful compound eyes one or more simple eyes (ocelli). It is not yet clearly understood how these extra eyes serve the insects. They seem capable of determining only the difference be-

tween dark and light, and experiments show that they are
of no use in guiding insects ; therefore they appear unneces-
sary, at all events for those which have a good pair of eyes as
well, unless they have some
use not yet discovered. It
is worth noticing that all
night-flying moths have ocelli.
The eyes of insect larvæ are
all simple ; not one species
possesses compound eyes until
it is mature ; therefore these
simple eyes belonged to the
old types of insects from which
the more highly developed
forms have sprung. The
ocelli are placed in a different
position to the eyes—sometimes at the top of the head,
or forward on the forehead, so
that they always look in a
different direction from the
eyes, for the true eyes are
usually at the side of the head.

SAWFLY LARVA SHOWING SIMPLE
EYES
Hugh Main

Being capable of distinguish-
ing dark from light, the ocelli can at least perceive a shadow,
so they may act as a warning on the approach of an enemy.
But no experiments have satisfactorily proved their value to
the species which still cling to them even after developing
compound eyes.

As to what appeals to insects' senses through their eyes,
we have first to consider colour. As the flowers which are

107

fertilized by insects show every shade of every colour known, it is only reasonable to suppose that these colours are to direct and attract the particular species which will perform this kindly act in the most satisfactory manner. Not that the insect any more than the flower is conscious of the deeper meaning of its mechanical actions. To the insect that colour and that scent suggest food or some other pressing need ; to the flower the putting forth of that colour and that scent follows on the ripening of the pollen as a matter of course, but the sense-organs of the insect are impressed by that particular flower, so that it passes by the colours and scents which are put out by other flowers.

The insect's eye, then, is set, so to speak, to catch a particular colour, and through the eye that colour impresses a certain nerve. This causes certain actions to be repeated mechanically every time that colour meets the eye—but we shall have more to say of this later on.

Lord Avebury made very interesting experiments with bees to prove their sense of colour. By comparing the results of a number of tests he was able to make a list of colours in the order in which they impress themselves on a hive-bee's eyes. He found that his bees always chose blue from among a variety of colours ; the next favourite—if blue was absent—was white ; then came green, orange, red, and lastly yellow. He proved, too, that the bees were guided by colour rather than by scent, and that they have a definite colour memory, and will not make a mistake when once a particular colour is fixed in their memory even if it is not their favourite colour. He did this by making little glass slides, each with a different coloured paper showing through ;

he then put a little honey on each and watched the bees' behaviour. One which chose a blue plate to feed off returned to it every time, and although an orange plate was put in its place she would not touch that honey, but searched for her blue plate until she found it. Another bee fed first off a red plate, no other being in sight, and after a few visits, when she was used to the idea that this colour meant honey, the red plate was taken away and replaced by a blue plate of honey, an empty red plate being put near it. The bee went first to the empty red plate, and spent some time examining it to see whether it really was honeyless ; then she actually flew away without discovering the honey on the blue plate. This shows very clearly that bees have a definite colour-memory, and that they are guided by colour rather than by scent, else she would surely have found the honey although it was associated with another colour.

We can follow out the meaning of this. Watch the bees at work visiting the flowers, and you will not fail to discover that one bee will confine itself to one kind of flower for the whole morning, or even for the whole day. Supposing a bee starts with blue flowers, it will continue visiting the same flowers for a definite period, though this does not prevent the same bee, when it has taken home its load of pollen or honey and cleaned itself thoroughly, paying a series of visits to mignonette flowers. In this manner the pollen of flowers is not wasted on species which it cannot fertilize ; the bee's colour-memory secures it from making mistakes.

Wasps' vision is not quite the same as that of bees. Experiments by another naturalist seem to show that wasps have a memory for form, which bees do not possess so acutely, and that they are more readily guided by smell than by colour-sense. Their memory for places and other things is more advanced than that of bees, and they are altogether more intelligent, and not such slaves of instinct.

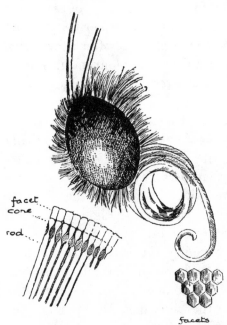

facet
cone
rod

facets

COMPOUND EYE OF BUTTERFLY

To test the sight of butterflies a very amusing experiment was once carried out by a scientist in America. Choosing a day when certain butterflies were flying about in numbers and were very active, he tied up some paper models of butterflies and let them flutter in the breeze. Some of these models were painted as accurately as possible, but others were purposely made too big or the wrong colour or the wrong shade of colour. The real butterflies were quite taken in, and flew round to make the acquaintance of the newcomers. They discovered the inaccuracies of the badly painted models when they were *three feet distant from them*, and would not make any friendly advances to these frauds, but they actually flirted with the well-painted ones, there being as many as six at one time making love to one painted female butterfly!

A butterfly's eye is compound, like those of many of the higher insects. There are a great number of lenses, and wonderful work has been done on the eye of a Tortoiseshell Butterfly to test exactly what it is capable of taking in by its organ of sight. The Tortoiseshell has six to seven thousand lenses on each side. Each lens is on the top of a little crystal cone, wider above and carried to a point at the bottom, so that it can collect the rays of light which strike the lens and concentrate them on the point; this leads into a long, slender tube, and below this are the nerves and muscles.

It used to be thought that eyes of this type reflected a number of tiny images, each lens registering a separate image, but the vision of these eyes is much more sharp and clear than it could ever be by such a method. In reality the rays of light are reflected into the cones each from one certain point of whatever the butterfly is looking at : the result being as many spots of colour as there are lenses. These spots together build up the picture. This is called the mosaic type of vision. But it must not be thought that the parts of the picture are visibly separated. As an insect's compound eyes are not flat, but rounded, each lens catches a different spot from the others, and the picture, pieced together, forms a continuous image very much like that which we see ourselves, though it is not so clear.

When the eye of a newly killed butterfly is taken out and all the muscles scraped away from below the little tubes, a perfect little camera is formed, and if this is set in a drop of glycerine an image may be seen reflected in it which gives a better idea of what the butterfly can really see than any amount of experiments. The picture thus reflected, though not quite sharp, gives every detail, and, more wonderful still, if this little camera is turned to a distant view the whole landscape will be cast on the glycerine quite distinctly. This is really amazing, and greatly astonished the first scientists who discovered it, for it has been proved that butterflies do not notice anything more than nine feet away, and as we have just remarked they only discovered the inaccuracies of the paper models when they were three feet distant from them. But the instrument for seeing distant objects is quite perfect ; it is only the butterfly's *intelligence* which is not far enough developed to use its instrument. It can see quite sufficient for its everyday needs, so as to detect the flowers which contain its food, or its mate, or its enemies, or the right plants to deposit its eggs on (though smell helps it mainly here) ; further than that is not necessary. Of what advantage would it be to a butterfly to perceive some distant hills, or even an enemy some way off ? Therefore it does not see the objects which actually come within its field of vision. They make an image on its eye, but it does not notice them, because it does not know what it is looking at. These objects have no direct concern in its daily life, and so the butterfly is not even conscious that they exist.

CHAPTER VIII

HOW INSECTS BREATHE

LIKE ourselves, all insects depend upon oxygen to keep them alive. The force which works all their delicate and complicated organs is heat, and to produce heat in their bodies before all things oxygen is necessary. But instead of being furnished with special breathing organs like our lungs, through which blood must pass in order to come in contact with oxygen, insects have quite another system ; the whole body of the insect is like one breathing organ, for the blood is always supplied with oxygen ; wherever there is blood there is oxygen as well. Tubes of air (trachæ) form a network all over the body, carrying oxygen to every organ, branching off into slender tubes which end in still finer ones like hairs, so that even the extreme tip of each limb is reached, and the smallest and most delicate organs are penetrated. The walls of these air-tubes allow the air to escape between the narrow rings of chitin which serve to strengthen them, while the tiny hair-like tubes are of thinner skin, through which the air passes freely.

All the muscles are provided with tiny air-tubes, for they, of course, require oxygen to work them, and because the delicate tubes might break when the muscle expanded they run up in a zigzag line which straightens as the muscle is stretched and returns to a spiral when it contracts again.

H

The main openings, spiracles, by which air enters, are on the two sides of an insect's body, and are closed by wonderful little valves of various designs which let in air and yet keep out any matter such as dust which might injure the organs. These little valves are quite an interesting study in themselves, there are so many different forms found among them.

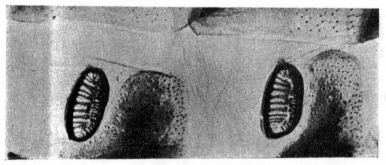

SPIRACLES OF WATER-BEETLE
Hugh Main

Some are shaped like lips pressed together; often the air has to pass a little grating of hairs before it reaches the tube, so that it is impossible for any small particles of dust to pass through without being held up. These valves or spiracles are formed to remain open, but there are muscles which are worked from inside to close them when it is necessary; directly the muscles release them the spiracles fall open again. If they always remained open the fresh air would fill the big tubes, but would only pass slowly into the little tubes, and these are very important to the insect, because they keep up the supply of oxygen for the organs which are using it up whenever they are active. So the manner in which an insect breathes is to close the spiracles and press a

114

little ring on to the larger air-tubes ; this forces the air which is in them through to the smallest tubes, after which the ring releases them, and more air passes from outside through the spiracles, which are now open again.

If you hold up a grasshopper or a dragonfly larva, and watch the movements of the soft part of its body, you will notice that each joint is expanding and contracting again like bellows, showing the movement of the muscles each time the insect takes in its air supply.

Insects do not require much oxygen at ordinary times when they breathe, but when they are making any special exertion, such as flying, or when they are feeding up at certain times, such as before pupating or pairing or egg-laying, and when they are most active in hot weather, then they use up more oxygen than at ordinary times, and then, of course, they require a larger supply. That is why those insects that spend much of their time in flying have, in addition to the usual air-tubes, little bladders of air in connexion with them ; these act as reservoirs to hold an extra supply of oxygen to make up for what is being used by the wings. These reservoirs are largest in dragonflies, moths, flies, and bees.

There is not much variety in the breathing apparatus of insects which live on land, but when we consider those that are found living in water we at once come across a multitude of different forms of breathing organs. Some carry pumps and siphons ; some wear diving-suits ; and others make cases which they fill with air and inside which they live. The large water-beetle which is so common in ponds and lakes, the Dytiscus Beetle, has its body covered on the upper side with a thick coat of very fine short hairs like velvet, and these hairs are set so close together that water cannot get between them, but the air can penetrate them, and remains en-

FEMALE MARGINED WATER-BEETLE
Hugh Main

tangled, forming a sheet of air-bubbles while the beetle is under water which is covered by the wing-cases. The beetle uses up this store of air by taking it in through the spiracles, and when the supply is nearly exhausted he may be seen to swim up to the surface of the water and, pushing the end of his body through the water-film, re-new the air-supply in the velvet under his wing-cases.

Our largest water-beetle, Hydrophilus, called the Silver Water-beetle, is not such a common species. This has velvet on the under-side of the body as well as under the wing-cases. We are able to see the lower air-supply as the beetle swims about under the water: the bubbles entangled in the velvet, being fused, look exactly like a shining sheet of metal.

HYDROPHILUS, THE GREAT
WATER-BEETLE

The Boatman has overdone his air-supply, and carries so much about with him entangled in his velvet that he is too light to remain below water unless he is rowing or has

116

anchored himself to something solid. Directly he leaves go he is carried by his own bubbles straight up to the top of the water. The Boatman is not a beetle, but belongs to the large order of beaked insects, and has instead of jaws a horny beak ending in a very sharp point, which pierces the creatures

WATER BOATMAN
Hugh Main

NYMPH, DRAGONFLY
Hugh Main

it feeds upon and sucks out their body-juices. Boatmen can dart about very quickly under water, aided by their velvet coat full of air-bubbles.

We have now to consider the larvæ of water-insects, and it is among these that the most delightful contrivances for getting oxygen are to be found.

There are several distinct methods used. There are the larvæ which breathe through spiracles in the way we have just been studying, or which have various ingenious little pumps to send air through the body. There are other

117

larvæ which have no spiracles, or if they have them keep them tightly closed under water ; these have special organs, called gills, covered with such thin skin that the oxygen from the water passes through them and so keeps the

GNAT LARVA
Hugh Main

air-tubes always supplied. Sometimes these gills are feathery, and sometimes like long hairs, or else like thin leaves. The feathery kind are the most beautiful, as in the mayfly larvæ. One can pick out some of the insects that are furnished with gills, because they keep them in constant movement, waving them up and down to send a current of water with a fresh quantity of oxygen through the slender tips. This movement is made because by this method of breathing less oxygen is extracted at a time from the water than when it is taken in direct from the outside air ; therefore the insect lives from hand to mouth, as it were, on its oxygen-supply, instead of having a reserve stock to draw from.

Those larvæ which live in semi-transparent tubes may be seen inside them undulating the whole body at short intervals to keep up a flow of water through the tube.

The siphons and pumps are of very fanciful designs, and though some are quite simple they show an extraordinary number of different schemes for attaining the same object. Perhaps the most fascinating is the breathing organ of the Chameleon Fly's larva, a curious little creature, shaped rather like a long, slender pod, which is not uncommon in ponds and ditches. Its tiny head is sometimes quite withdrawn out of sight and sometimes pushed out to look for food. The mouth is principally a bunch of hooks. To breathe in air it puts its tail through the water-film and spreads out an organ the shape of the top of a sweep's brush ; this is formed of long, branched hairs which hold back the water, making a little depression in the film at the surface, to bring the air down to the spiracle in the centre of this circular brush.

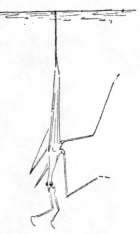

LONG WATER SCORPION TAKING IN AIR THROUGH ITS SIPHON

Very beautiful are the larvæ of one of the big Hover-flies, called by the uncouth name of Rat-tailed Maggot. At the end of the body are curious flexible tubes which can be elongated to a length ten times that of the body. The larvæ feed on dead leaves at the bottom of shallow pieces of water, and are to be found often in water-butts. Where the water is not too deep they can enjoy a meal at the bottom while their long siphons are sent to the top of the water and opened up to the air. So they are pumping in oxygen at the same time as feeding, which is a very satisfactory time-saving arrangement.

Gnat larvæ also have siphons at the end of the body, but these cannot be lengthened, so they have to wriggle themselves to the top of the water whenever they need oxygen.

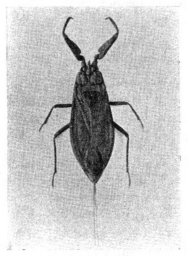

WATER SCORPION
Hugh Main

Among siphons, those of the Water Scorpions are of a very nice pattern, being formed of two pieces which fit together so beautifully that no air escapes when it is sent through to the spiracles from the surface. When the scorpion leaves the water the two pieces of the siphon part so that air can pass straight to the spiracles at the end of its body.

CHAPTER IX

WINGS AND FLIGHT

OTHER groups in the animal kingdom besides insects are able to fly, and it may be thought that the study of the structure of wings in one group would give us knowledge of how wings develop in the other groups, but when we look into the formation of an insect's wing we find it such a totally different organ of flight from that of a bird or bat, for instance, that we can make very little comparison between them—except that all wings have to serve a common purpose, namely, to carry their respective owners through the air.

Birds and bats have developed the art of flying to a very high degree of excellence ; their whole structure has been adapted to make flying possible. Their first pair of limbs have become modified in the course of ages into wings, with light, jointed bones, covered with plumes, and the very strong muscles by which the wings are spread or folded or turned in any direction are firmly attached to the breast-bone.

But insects have no inner skeleton, as birds and animals have, to give support to their limbs. All their soft, delicate organs are inside the body, surrounded by hard rings and plates of the tough outer skin (chitin), with thinner skin between them so that the plates are movable. To this chitin all the limbs of an insect are attached by strong muscles which work in the same way as do backboned animals' muscles, except that in backboned animals the muscles which work the outside limbs are under the skin and covered with soft flesh, while in insects this is reversed, the soft parts being inside and the muscles attached outside to the chitin, which thus takes the place of an inner skeleton.

WALL BUTTERFLIES
One just out of chrysalis case and one mature.
Hugh Main

It might be imagined that this kind of structure would present so many difficulties that no adequate means of flight could be developed, but insects are used to making a success out of seeming impossibilities, and the organs of flight which they have evolved are very efficient, and some of the groups of insects contain very powerful and expert flyers.

Insects' wings actually grow out of the layer of skin underneath the chitin, and push through the outer skin in the form of little buds. When we look into the structure of the fully developed wing of a butterfly it is a surprise to find that it is

122

strong enough to bear the insect, light though it is, the chief support being from rods of chitin which branch out from the base and from the muscles which are attached to the chitin inside the thorax (these are the only muscles which are inside the chitin instead of being fastened to the exterior).

Butterflies and moths interlock the fore and hind pairs of wings lightly at the base, so that they are like one pair. This interlocking mechanism varies. Sometimes it takes the form of a bunch of bristles on the hind-wing which catch into a little flap on the fore-wing, or instead of bristles there may be a small hook, or the edge of the fore-wing may turn over and catch in the hind-wing.

PUPAL WINGS OF LARGE WHITE BUT-
TERFLY, WHICH ARE USUALLY SEEN
GLUED AGAINST THE SIDE OF THE
PUPA
Hugh Main

In flying insects the fore-wings are usually larger than the hind pair (except in Caddis-flies, and these do not rank with the best fliers.

Wasps and bees and their relations have a more ingenious arrangement for locking the two pairs of wings ; this consists of a row of little twisted hooks on the front edge of the hind-wing which can be slipped over a ridge on the hind edge of the fore-wing. They work quite freely, and have been described as " slipping to and fro like rings on the rod of a window-curtain."

Some of the two-winged insects are far superior to those of the other orders in the matter of using their wings. Notice 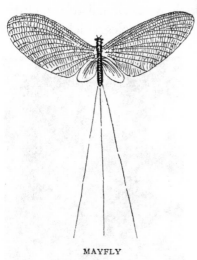 the graceful and intricate dancing of flies on the ceiling, the swiftness with which they turn and swerve without ever making a mistake or coming into collision, or watch a Hover - fly in the sunshine poised over the flowers, supported in that position by such rapid vibrations of the wings as to make them invisible, darting at a blossom and then away like a zigzag streak of colour,

MAYFLY

or try to catch a bluebottle even at close quarters in a small room, and see the almost incredible swiftness with which it can double and dodge, and you will soon be convinced that flies have brought the art of flying to a wonderful stage of perfection. But we must make one exception when we state that two-winged

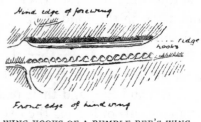

WING-HOOKS OF A BUMBLE-BEE'S WING

insects can manipulate their wings better than those with two pairs; the exception is the dragonfly, especially the Demoiselle, which, in spite of having a long body to balance, and sometimes using both pairs of wings as one pair, some-

124

times using each pair independently of the other, is one of the prettiest and most agile flyers of all winged insects.

Beetles only use one pair of wings ; the fore pair has developed into a horny cover (elytra) under which the thin, gauzy pair is tidily folded away when not in use. The edges of the elytra are often used for packing up the wings. In some species the cover is quite short, as for example, in the Rove Beetles, whose wings take up so little space when not being used that the long body is almost entirely exposed, instead of being covered by the elytra. These beetles have a wonderful system of packing up the netted pair, and it is a beautiful sight to watch Creophilus—the grey and black soft-bodied beetle commonly found under dead birds and animals in company with the Burying Beetle—putting away its long wings after a flight. The wings when spread out stretch beyond the body, the tip of which bends back to make the first fold in the wings ; after this two knobby processes on the thorax are brought into action and the wings pressed against them in such a manner that they fold up in their original creases, the whole operation being carried out so quickly and easily as to leave one breathless. The long, delicate wings have vanished completely under the neat little covers which look like an unpretentious little knapsack flung over the beetle's shoulder.

By far the most elaborate method of folding wings is that adopted by earwigs. Their wings first fold up in pleats like a fan, and then are folded again, with sometimes just a tiny corner left visible as if it could not be fitted in. It is a wonderful system of folding, but takes rather longer to carry out than that of Creophilus.

Stick insects, locusts, and Praying Mantises also have wings which fold fanwise, but they do not have to exert themselves at all, because usually the elytra are the same length as the wings, and the muscles manage the folding without any assistance from any other part of the body.

All insects' wings begin their growth as a chain of cells which develop from the cells of the skin under the chitin ;

LOCUST

Hugh Main

these form a rounded lump, which gradually pushes itself through the surface, and while a larva is growing these wing-buds are growing too. In some caterpillars they can even be seen after the third moult as small swellings on the thorax, sometimes spotted. The wing-growth does not entirely fill this swelling, but is folded and crumpled ; this leaves a space around it which is very important, for when the caterpillar is changing into a pupa the protecting sheath of the wing-growth turns back, and the blood presses in to fill the spaces. Thus the supply of blood for the growing wings is started. Every organ is supplied with air as well as blood, and in wings this is, of course, particularly necessary. Directly the first growth of the wing-buds is begun they are supplied with air by fine branches of the larger air-tubes of the body which push up into the new growth ; later, when the wings have expanded into two layers of thin skin pressed together, the ends of these air-tubes develop into veins, which may be seen in any insect's wings lying between the two layers of skin. Wings are therefore made up of two thin layers of skin supported by veins which strengthen them and at the same time, being filled with air, help to make them light.

Insects' blood circulates through the wings, and as it drives its course comes in contact with oxygen and then flows back through the body ; so for this reason wings may be considered as extra breathing organs, because in them the blood becomes aerated.

The arrangements of the veins of the wings vary very considerably in different kinds of insects. Some wings, such as those of the nerve-winged insects, are covered all over with a network of branched veins crossed by finer ones ; other wings, such as those of the greenfly, have very few veins. The arrangement of the veins is of very great importance when one is trying to identify an insect, and anyone wishing to make himself really familiar with the different types should certainly devote some time to studying the wings.

It will be noticed that in no insect are the wings inserted quite straight in the thorax—they always start backward a little ; nor are the joints on which they turn quite straight—they are set in the socket at an angle, so that the strokes made by the wings are not level, horizontal strokes backward and forward. For the ordinary stroke in flight is exactly like the stroke of an oar in rowing, being first forward and upward, then turning slightly, then backward and downward. The reason for this is the same as in rowing ; the forward stroke cuts through the air in front ; if the backward stroke returned on the same plane no advance would be made, but the backward stroke, meeting the air which has thus been set in motion, carries the insect forward, just as the boat is propelled forward by the oar-blade pushing against the resisting water. A curved surface offers more resistance than a flat one, which is the reason why oars are not flat ; insects' wings, though flatter than those of bats or birds, are still slightly convex above and concave below. As the wing moves forward and slightly upward the underside is the more exposed, and on the return stroke this concave surface is used against the resistance of the air, so that the wings seem to spoon up the air and push it behind the insect at every stroke. This is called the figure-of-eight curve, but we must remember to picture our figure formed of elliptical curves and not perfect ones, for the wings make a short curve before the return stroke.

Insects' wings move at such a rate that it would be impossible to guess exactly how they work and what sort of curve they are making in the air ; but this has been carefully worked out by some very clever experiments. Live insects were fastened lightly to a surface without hurting them or impeding the action of their wings. Strips of blackened paper were fixed on a revolving cylinder at the side, and as the tips of the wings just touched it the vibrations were registered, and the wing-beats calculated more or less accurately. Some allowance must, of course, be made for the slight diminishing of speed owing to the wings coming in contact with the paper, so that the number of wing-beats per second probably really exceeds that which is recorded, but the comparison between the different flying insects, as

128

well as the extraordinarily high number of beats which a fly is able to make is of great interest.

	Wing-beats per second
Common fly	330
Drone fly	240
Bee	190
Wasp	110
Humming-bird moth	72
Dragonfly	28
White Butterfly	9

This table just proves how necessary it is that experiments should be made wherever it is possible in order to prove the truth of any point. Supposing those who had given some serious study to the subject of flight were asked to guess the number of wing-beats made by various flying insects ; it is highly improbable that their numbers would have come anywhere near those which have been found by actual experiment.

The idea of the figure-of-eight movement of the wings was also the result of a valuable experiment. A captured wasp had the tip of the front wing painted with gold leaf ; it was then liberated and carefully observed flying in the sun, when the movement of its vibrating wings could distinctly be seen to take this curve. While the insect is in the air the body is not rigid, but is of considerable help in making sudden turns by throwing the weight in a different direction. Such small details are of great importance ; and when we realize the marvellous powers of flight in the insect world, the absolute command insects have over their wings, so that they can turn, hover, stop, drop to the ground, and even in some cases *reverse* without ever coming to grief, we must admit that all these small details are carried out with the utmost exactitude.

The movements or vibrations of insects' wings are characteristically backward and forward strokes, while the movements of bats' and birds' wings are more in an up and down direction. Butterflies move their wings with strokes which are more up and down than those of any other flying insect, though not completely so. The movement, too, which propels them differs from that of other orders of insects, because when the upward stroke is nearly finished the wings separate, and the fore-wing partly overlaps the hind-wing toward the end of the down stroke. All insects' wings, of whatever shape they may be, are angular, though the angles themselves are not sharp, but rounded off ; and as the wing is slightly twisted in the socket, when an insect turns in the air sometimes a part of both the upper and the lower surface is opposed to the resisting air. This is especially noticeable in a dragonfly's wings.

In spite of their triumphant mastery over the problems of flight which have baffled the human race for ages, insects are still at the mercy of air-currents, and being so light are carried away to very long distances. This is sometimes of great advantage to us human beings as, for instance, when a locust swarm is carried out to sea ; it also accounts for insects being found on islands very far from the mainland. There are other means of transit, such as drifting logs or floating masses of vegetation, but in many cases the colonization of remote islands by certain types of insects may be due to strong winds against which their wonderful powers of flight are used in vain.

CHAPTER X

STINGS AND POISONS

STINGING is a business which is carried out seriously by comparatively few insects. Real stings consist of a slender, pointed instrument capable of puncturing; connected with this is a bag of strong acid, which has the effect of paralysing the victim. The act of puncturing sets in motion a series of muscles, and results in the poison from the bag running into the wound. Among insects the train of muscular actions following on a sting is entirely mechanical; that is to say, a stinging insect cannot prevent the poison flowing when once its sting drives home. Spiders are thought to possess the power of withholding the poison when they bite, and it is possible that scorpions can also command their stings in the same manner, sometimes making a clean puncture, with no worse effects following than those from a needle-prick. This question, however, has not been satisfactorily proved.

But stinging insects always mean to sting, and do not change their mind half-way through the operation. Bees and wasps are first-class stingers; so also are some kinds of ants which have stings and poison bags complete. The effect of a sting varies according to whether the victim is in full vigour or not, and depends also upon whether the blood is in a fit state to resist poison and upon the depth of the puncture—all this, of course, relating to a human victim ; and it varies according to the size and natural protection of an insect victim.

Some of the parasitic wasps, called Ophion Flies, are capable of giving us a very sharp sting, though the effect of it is usually neither so lasting nor so severe as that of bees and wasps. These Ophion Flies have curious curved bodies unlike those of any other insect, and the females have long ovipositors, plainly to be seen, more than half the length of the body. The Ophions we are most familiar with in England are medium-sized, yellow-red in colour, and often come in at open windows in summer, attracted by lights, in which they will commit suicide if given the opportunity. They fly with a curious gliding movement as if they were sailing. It is the females which sting with their sharp-tipped ovipositor ; they seldom attack, but if interfered with can make themselves respected. Their attitude when stabbing is exactly that of a stinging insect. Other insects armed with sharp ovipositors but no poison do not use them in defence, and do not take this particular attitude.

Our British Ophions are not of any considerable size, but anybody who has bred out Wild Silk Moths from North America is familiar with the large and handsome Ophion which to our chagrin so often emerges from those cocoons instead of the expected moth.

These insects are a reddish amber in colour, with turquoise-blue eyes, but the females should be handled with caution. One which I was holding idly by the wings to watch how she could bend her lithe body in any direction brought her ovipositor to an angle that enabled her to give me a sudden stab on the tip of the thumb, and the wound, though very tiny, ached for more than twenty-four hours afterward.

It is well known that the stings of a nest of infuriated wasps can kill a horse, but even one sting can sometimes produce serious results in a human being ; a sting on the head has been known to cause unconsciousness.

It is often said that mosquitoes sting, but this is quite wrong. In the first place it is the sharp-pointed mouth-parts of the mosquito which make the wound, and secondly, although an irritating fluid flows into the wound, it is not of the same nature as the poison we have just discussed ; nobody was ever rendered unconscious by the bite of a mosquito.

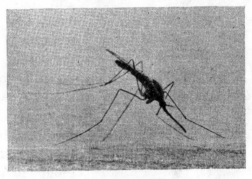

MALARIAL MOSQUITO
Hugh Main

Mosquitoes live upon fluids ; therefore their mouths are not of the biting type, such as those of grasshoppers, beetles, or caterpillars, etc., which have mouths for biting off small solid fragments. Mosquitoes' mouth-parts consist of a very slender tube, long enough to reach the blood, with a sharp point for piercing the skin, and a pump. The fluid which flows into the wound is what is called an irritant, and its use is to make blood flow to the spot where the tube has been

133

driven in, so that the mosquito may get a good feed with the least trouble.

Blood-poisoning by insects is a very different matter from stinging. It is caused by insects carrying to our blood some sort of matter which is foreign to it and so setting up inflammation. Flies are said to have poisonous stings, but the truth is that in puncturing our skin they sometimes carry into the wound portions of what they were last feeding upon. As flies are not very particular in their choice of food, the result can be a bad case of blood-poisoning. But it cannot be said of flies that they are stinging insects.

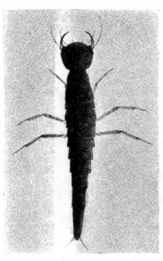

DYTISCUS BEETLE LARVA
Hugh Main

Here and there among the groups of insects we find fluids which produce poisonous effects. Some of the beaked insects have a poisonous bite. The American species of this group are called Assassin Bugs, from their habit of stabbing insect prey which are paralysed by the poisoned stroke. When human beings get a bite from these insects the wound is always very painful, and may be serious.

In other insects the fluid following a bite is not of a paralysing nature, but has a digestive property, and kills the victim by changing its body-juices into a form which needs no further digestion.

The curious grub of the Dytiscus Beetle is one of these.

134

Its sickle-shaped jaws are hollow, and pointed at the tips. They seize the victim and pierce the skin ; and their jaws being hollow the body - juices are sucked through them. But the death of the victim takes place sooner than it would if caused simply by loss of blood, because a fluid flows from the grub's mouth and acts on the blood, digesting it. It is a very practical time-saving system on the part of the grub, but gives the victims no chance of escape when once caught in those cruel jaws ; they are usually soft

GLOW-WORM LARVA FEEDING
Hugh Main

creatures, such as other insect grubs, or tadpoles, or earthworms. So also with glow-worms, who feed on snails, reaching them inside their shells by their long, thin body and small head. Here they put out a strong acid from their mouth, which converts the soft body of the snail into a digestible form before the glow-worm begins to feed.

CHAPTER XI

INSTINCT

WHEN we look carefully into the doings of insects and study the laws that they obey, it is quite easy to make mistakes about their intelligence, for some of their actions are so astoundingly clever that it seems as if the insect must know what it is doing, and that it must be able to think out what will be the best way out of a difficulty, the most successful plan for outwitting an enemy, or the surest scheme for providing for the future. But on the other hand we have many instances of how extraordinarily stupid an insect can be if it is put off its beat ; so that at one moment we are sure insects have more intelligence than many of the higher animals—including man—and at the next moment we are equally sure that they are nothing but little machines.

The reason for this seeming contradiction is quite simple. Most of their marvellous doings can be traced to instinct, which has reached a higher degree of perfection among insects than in any other group of the animal kingdom. If insects act solely by instinct, the result is that if anything happens to upset the order of events which their instincts have trained them to follow they will be either utterly thrown out and unable to act at all or, as often happens, will continue stupidly to follow out their usual course of action, even if the chief event on which all the other actions depend has not taken place.

For example, the female Digger Wasp prepares a larder with every egg she lays, fitting up the mud cell first with the egg, then with food, and finally sealing the cell. The insects which compose this larder have to be caught and stung so that they are paralysed, then dragged to the cell, so that the larva may have an insect to feed upon when it hatches. Experiments show that if the egg be taken out of the cell the wasp will not notice it has gone, but will continue her preparations to the smallest detail, bring a paralysed insect, place it in the cell, and seal this up, without understanding that the very object for which all this trouble is being taken is not there !

Here is a case of an insect's action which might seem contradictory ; if we consider that the wasp *understands* all the wonderful preparation she is making for the future welfare of her larva, then we must think that she acts with astonishing stupidity in not discovering that her egg is stolen. But if we call her action *instinctive*, then we find that the course of events has not been disturbed by the theft, and one action will prompt the next quite mechanically until the final sealing up of the cell.

We noticed on page 69 that the Praying Mantis which mimics a blossom will actually reject branches bearing buds or fruit, and select one in bloom, before taking up her attitude of floral mimicry ; and yet this same mantis, if she should happen to remain unfertilized during the breeding season, will still toil over the construction of her wonderful nest, and possibly build up three such during that period, each

137

containing rows and rows of little, empty eggs, from which, alas! not one little mantis will ever emerge.

Then, again, we have the wonderful instinct of moths and butterflies, which, although they themselves feed on nectar, will select a plant which is the food of their caterpillars, and lay their eggs upon it. But if the juice of that plant can be extracted, and some other plant soaked in it (as has been done with mustard oil, which is the juice of plants on which some of the Cabbage White Butterflies feed), then the butterflies will just as readily lay their eggs on that plant, although it does not happen to be the food of their caterpillars.

In this case, thanks to the interesting experiments just referred to, it is clear that it is the scent of a particular plant, acting upon the scent-organs of the butterfly, which sets going a whole series of complicated machinery, ending in the laying of eggs. It is instinct which guides the action of insects ; but what, then, is instinct and how do instincts begin ?

All instincts have their starting-point in one or other of the sense-organs—organs of smell, sight, hearing, touch, taste. Anything which excites these sense-organs affects the nerve-bundles which in insects take the place of a brain. The nerves direct certain movements of muscles in response to these excitations of the sense-organs, and as these movements are repeated every time that particular sense-organ is affected, a habit is formed which may be inherited. The actions may be added to by the next generation ; and that is how these wonderful instincts are gradually built up.

Sense-organs are the doors by which anything outside ourselves is brought to our notice : all things enter our consciousness by means of our five senses. Sense-organs are the means of communication between any creature and its surroundings. Even so lowly a creature as the amœba has the sense of touch ; otherwise it would not expand when its way is clear, and retract when it encounters an obstacle, and flow over the particles which form its food.

If any creature were deprived of all its senses—sight, hearing, taste, touch, smell—it would be imprisoned in itself and completely cut off from the outside world, and however clever it was, and however much brain it possessed, that would be of no help to it, because no new ideas could come to it except through the sense-organs.

Light and heat work on insects and produce various actions that are necessary to their life, so they are very useful powers of excitation. Some insects at certain periods of their life develop a particular sensitiveness to light, which starts a whole series of actions dependent upon the excitation caused by light. Young caterpillars of the Goldtail Moth, which feed upon buds, or shoots, or young leaves, were discovered to be endued with that sensitiveness to light directly they start feeding after hibernation. This makes them climb upward toward the strongest light, until they reach the tip of the branches or top of the plant. There the scent-organ is acted upon by the scent of the food, and the caterpillar begins to feed. After its first meal there is no need for it to search for its food, so it is no longer guided by a craving for light.

The swarming of bees and ants has also been found to be guided by a craving for light. All sorts of ideas have been suggested to account for the strange fact that bees know when to swarm, and all in a moment, as if some signal had been given, rush out of the hive in perfect order. A scientist who had a glass observation hive in his laboratory made this interesting discovery by accident : he happened to hear his bees beginning to swarm inside, and took off the dark cover to watch their behaviour. There was a skylight just above the hive, and directly the light was let in on them the bees stopped pressing to the opening and surged back toward the light which was coming through their glass roof. By putting on the dark cover the bees were started again toward their opening, and again checked and brought back by taking it off. By this means the bees were actually prevented from swarming for the whole of that day, and gradually quieted down. The next day they went through exactly the same performance, but at last were allowed to swarm. This experiment makes it evident that this craving for light is developed in some swarming insects, and acts upon them so strongly that it forces them toward the lightest part of their nest, which in underground communities will be the opening. The other swarming instincts follow on this excitation caused by sensitiveness to light when once the insects have left the nest.

Besides these finished instincts which lead insects to carry out such marvellous pieces of work in such a faultless fashion, there is another power which has carried the insect world through a great deal of trouble, and that is the ability to answer to quite new excitations and so form new habits which may be very useful to them in the great competition of all creatures for a little corner of their own in this universe. By repetition these responses to a new experience of the sense-organs become crystallized into habits, so that a succeeding generation will respond by instinct to an excitation to which their ancestors were probably quite indifferent.

Instincts are sufficient for any creature so long as they meet all the common requirements of its life, particularly those concerned with the future generations. These are the chief anxiety of insects, and we find the most highly developed instincts are all concerned with what affects them.

Instincts are sufficient for the needs of most insects, but there are some, and especially the social insects, which have to face problems for which no inherited instinct can prepare them. These insects have developed an intelligence of a higher order, which is a step on toward the brain-power of the more advanced types of animals.

Ants, wild bees, and wasps are reckoned as the most intelligent insects, because among them we find all sorts of qualities which cannot come under the heading of instincts, such as resourcefulness in dealing with problems, ingenuity, memory, perseverance, and the ability to be taught by experience.

The outside work of insect colonies creates problems which need a higher sense than instinct to deal with them, and perhaps the workers of ant colonies have the greatest need of all, because they are wingless. Certainly it is among ant workers that we find the most highly developed nerves.

Instinct can direct all the actions which take place inside an ant's nest, by which the eggs are fertilized, laid, tended until they hatch ; and the larvæ are fed, cleaned, defended, and given material to spin their cocoon—if they make one ; and the pupæ are cleaned and kept in the right temperature until the mature ant is ready to emerge ; and the pupal skin is peeled off them and their limbs are straightened out for them by their devoted attendants, and they are set on their legs, henceforward to take their place as working members of the commonwealth. Instinct can direct all these actions. But when we consider the activities of those ants which work outside the nest we discover the need of another order of intelligence.

All day long lines of wingless workers are hurrying up and down their highroads, worn smooth by thousands of little feet, bringing food for the colony. As all the fetching and carrying is done on foot, so to speak, the first consideration is economy of time and energy if the strength of the colony is to be kept up. So scouts are sent out in all directions to quite a long distance from the nest to search for booty, and when anything good is discovered they will lay a scent-trail to it and fetch some of the workers to combine in carrying it home. Instinct teaches the workers to follow a scent-trail laid by their leaders, and how implicit is their obedience to this instinct may be tested by interrupting one of these foraging expeditions by drawing one's finger across the trail. Instantly the workers are thrown into confusion, the work is stopped, and they rush here and there quite aimlessly until the leaders have succeeded in repairing the breach by running over the trail where the new, strange scent had damaged it.

Observations on Army Ants in Nicaragua made by Belt, the famous naturalist, show very clearly the wisdom and judgment of the ant-leaders, and the unhesitating loyalty to their leadership of the workers. The food of Army Ants is mainly live insects ; they travel in massed formation hunting their prey, and overcome by their vast numbers any small creatures unlucky enough to be in their path. Everything flees in terror before the Army Ants.

One of these armies happened to be crossing a railway, and Belt noticed that every time a train passed thousands of these were crushed. But a little later when Belt observed them again there were no longer any ants on the lines; the army was marching through tunnels which they had made under the rails. Belt scraped away these tunnels, but it did not have the effect he expected; the ants only waited long enough to excavate new tunnels, for the leaders had sensed danger perhaps from the large numbers of corpses, and somehow the order had gone forth that no ant was to cross the rails. The leaders had started a new trail, and no ant would act contrary to their guidance.

A similar instance was noticed in Italy, when the observer who recorded it was watching streams of a small red species which came into a house through the windows. As the intruders were troublesome a fly-paper was stretched across the window-sill, and this was soon covered with hundreds of little ant-corpses. Next morning, however, there was no increase in the number of the dead, but a line of living ants was crossing the sticky surface quite unconcernedly, by a path which they had made of bits of soil, etc. Not only were they carrying out their original plan, but they were taking advantage of the flies and other insects that were caught on the paper, and dragging them away as food.

In the Insect House at the Zoo observations were made on the colony of wood ants established in one of the bays. These are the largest of our British ants, and

NEST OF GREAT WOOD ANT

Hugh Main

are found in fir-woods, where they build large nests of pine-needles.

Two colonies of these ants were started, each surrounded by a trench of water three inches broad, which formed a moat and prevented their escape. From time to time a dead mouse was given them as food, which was buried in a few days. It was always laid on the same piece of ground, but it happened on one occasion that while the ants were burying one it rolled over into the moat. Then a scene of confusion followed, for some of the ants fell in with it, and rescue-parties had to be sent out to them ; finally, as they could not recover the corpse of the mouse, it was removed, and another laid on identically the same spot. But this time there was a noticeable change in the ants' method of burying it, for they dug on one side of the mouse only, away from the water, so that it rolled down toward the nest. This was not directed by instinct, neither was it a coincidence, for mice were often given them, and always before this they had buried them in the same way, by digging directly under them. Clearly the leaders profited by the memory of their recent disaster and avoided a repetition of the accident, but this incident shows an intelligence not far removed from reasoning power.

As one of these ant colonies became overcrowded, a bridge was placed over the moat between the two nests, and they were allowed to fight and recolonize the ground. The pupæ of the conquered nest were stolen by the stronger colony, and, wishing to find out whether these were being put in the ordinary nurseries or were separated, the victors' nest was disturbed. The ants were in a very excitable state after

K

this recent battle, and poured out from all sides, looking for the new enemy.

No enemy being visible, they were rather at a loss what to

HEAD OF TIGER BEETLE LARVA AT TOP OF BURROW
Hugh Main

do next, but one soldier ant went down to the bridge-head and there stood sentinel for nearly half an hour, challenging every ant that crossed in either direction, interrogating all with his antennæ as to their business before they were allowed to proceed.

146

The interesting point about his independent action is that his chosen position was so astoundingly correct, for it was the only point at which an invading enemy could have entered their ground. They must have realized that the nest was surrounded by water, and that, except by air, when they would certainly have been warned by a shadow, the only accessible corner was the bridge.

One other interesting event occurred in connexion with the same ants when the larva of a Tiger Beetle was introduced into the colony. These larvæ dig burrows near ants' hills—but of smaller species than the wood ants—and feed on all the ants which fall into them. This larva was hastily placed in a hole on the bank near one of these ant colonies to prove whether he could tackle the larger species of ants. In a few minutes a patrolling soldier discovered the ugly, armoured head protruding from its burrow, and at once

TIGER BEETLE LARVA
TAKEN OUT OF
BURROW
Hugh Main

seized it and tried to drag it out. But the larva has a hook on its back which it fixes into the soil, and so was able to resist the efforts of five ants which collected to dislodge it. For nearly an hour the ants continued their efforts, but at the end of that time they suddenly changed their tactics, and two of them went to the back of the burrow and dug him out—forced him to emerge by biting his soft body— and carried him in triumph below.

These are only a few instances of the sagacity of ants, and

147

many more might be quoted to show that on occasions when ordinary instincts fail they have the sense to make new trials until one succeeds. This is the highest form of intelligence among insects, and, indeed, ranks quite high in a general comparison of the mental powers of all animals.

CHAPTER XII

CARAVANS AND SLEEPING-BAGS

WE have seen already that while the change from the grub to the adult is taking place many insects require a period of rest, which is more or less prolonged according to the importance of these structural changes. Insects which go through a quiescent pupal stage are defenceless during that period, but it must not be supposed that all their enemies are inactive. In the majority of species this period of rest coincides with the winter months or with the dry season, when the majority of predacious insects at least are dormant, but other enemies are on the prowl. We know that during our English winters many insectivorous birds remain with us, and these and the mammals which do not hibernate are glad of any form of insect diet.

So we find it a general rule that those insects which need a long period of rest need also special protection, which is for the most part accomplished by a covering which blends with their surroundings, and renders them inconspicuous to prying eyes. That is why caterpillars form a chrysalid or spin a cocoon, and flies wrap themselves in such a horny case against thieves that some of them have to be provided with a special organ on their heads to force their own front door.

The caterpillars of some moths weave such a tough envelope that they have to leave one end loose and soft, and

even then the emerging moth has to be furnished with a strong acid to melt the fibres or it would not be strong enough to push itself out. But besides its strength the appearance of a sleeping-bag is a very important factor in the safety of the owner ; it is for the most part of some neutral tint, such as brown, green, and grey. Some moths appear to be in the transition stage between those who remain naked pupæ and those which construct an elaborate cocoon. These economize in their covering by spinning a loose net through which the pupa is easily seen. But in these species also the pupa partakes of the colouring of its surroundings. There is a

SACK ON HEAD OF BLUE-BOTTLE FLY SWOLLEN OUT TO FORCE OFF FRONT END OF PUPARIUM

Hugh Main

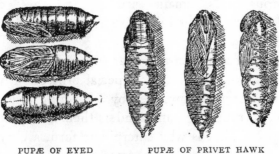

PUPÆ OF EYED HAWK MOTH

PUPÆ OF PRIVET HAWK MOTH

Peter Scott

group of Wild Silk Moths which has a brilliant green pupa lightly slung in a hammock of large-meshed netting, but

150

against green foliage the vivid tints of the pupa are neutralized, and from a distance the hammock will appear empty.

Many species pupate underground, especially beetles, and these are usually content with an earthen cell in the soil. In these cases protective coloration is ignored, and the pupa is

DIAMOND-BACKED MOTH COCOON
Hugh Main

usually white or cream, or a rich brown or almost black. The chief enemies of these sleeping insects are the tiny ones which creep down to them through chinks and holes. It does not much matter what coloured garb the victim wears, for it cannot save him from this type of foe.

PUPA OF STAG BEETLE
Hugh Main

Just a few beetle larvæ cover themselves with a loose, untidy case, but a covering is not necessary in the

151

timber or the soil where they usually rest, and most beetles simply turn into a pupa without any sort of covering.

There are many insects which make no particular preparation for transformation; they change their skin in public,

DYTISCUS BEETLE JUST EMERGED FROM
PUPAL SKIN
Hugh Main

and emerge forthwith, taking apparently very little trouble about it. Grasshoppers will hold on to a grass stem, split the nymphal skin, and are away without any fuss; and a gnat pupa will be seen dancing near the surface of the water one moment, and in the next it has wriggled itself free, spread its wings, and vanished.

Beetles, however, remain in their cells after the final transformation has taken place, so that the layers of chitin which cover them may harden, and butterflies must allow time for their delicate, crumpled wings to expand and be strengthened to bear them.

The chief material in the manufacture of cocoons is a

152

matter which exists in liquid form in glands in the insect's
body ; this fluid hardens when it comes in contact with the

EMPTY COCOON OF PUSS MOTH ON OAK
Hugh Main

air, and may be mixed with gum and massed into solid form
as an envelope, or may be pulled out as threads only, through a
little organ called the press, and woven into a matted blanket.

153

The Puss Moth Caterpillar makes a solid envelope, not making a thread, but using the silk in a gummy putty, and then covers this with tiny morsels of bark, bitten out of the trunk of the tree it feeds on. When this hardens it results in an exact facsimile of the irregular raised knots or ridges, and is well-nigh invisible. Some moths have blanket cocoons with a gummy finish which makes them leathery.

SAWFLY COCOONS ON HAWTHORN
Hugh Main

Sawfly grubs make this form of sleeping-bag as a general rule. There is one species, frequently found in this country on Scotch pines, which pupates on the tips of the branches in a cocoon which bears an extraordinary resemblance to the little, gummy buds.

The cocoons of some young ants are interesting, although such a sketchy affair that one can think of them only as a protective habit which has lost its significance. Only some species spin them. The tiny splinters of wood or plant-fibre are selected and brought by their diligent nurses; the larvæ are carried to a suitable spot, propped into a suitable attitude, and watched and waited upon while the operation is proceeding. One imagines that if the

154

nurses could spin the cocoons that labour too would be spared them.

The cases in which some grubs live during the whole of their larval existence are more interesting than cocoons, for they are caravans, movable houses, which they carry with

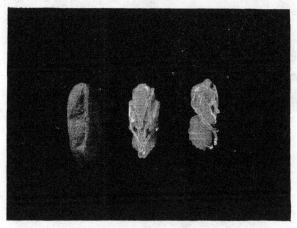

COCOON AND PUPÆ OF ANT

Hugh Main

them wherever their needs urge them. They are no doubt adopted as a protection against enemies, those grubs which use them being much sought after as food by other animals. It is well known that Caddis-worms form a good bait for fishes when taken out of their cases, and if they quit them voluntarily while in the water they are liable to be snapped up almost immediately. There is no doubt that the caravan spells safety for them.

It is amusing to watch a hungry Dytiscus Beetle trying to force an entrance into a Caddis case, tugging at the articles

155

with which it is hung like a tinker's caravan, biting at the tough silken lining ; he will probably have to go away disappointed, but fish, patiently awaiting their chance until

the unsuspecting grub shows itself, will often succeed in dislodging the inhabitant, and in maiming it by a blow on the head.

In very shallow stagnant pools, among a certain fine water - weed (*Spirogyra*), is found a little midge-grub which makes a tube not unlike a Caddis case. This case is composed of the weed itself, on which the grub feeds, partly digesting it, then mixing it into a sort of jelly, and with this moulding a tube to fit its own body, adding

COCOONS OF EMPEROR MOTH
One opened to show pupa and trapped door.
Hugh Main

the material bit by bit at either end until the tube is long enough to more than cover it. As a finishing touch fragments of green weed are worked into the outer side of the material, negligently, but with all the more artistic effect.

When seen under a lens the midge-grub seems to have fashioned a bower for itself, with tendrils of green hanging over the two entrances. Although where these midges are

156

found they occur in numbers they are difficult to discover, for to the naked eye they appear as little bladders which might easily be the seed-pods of some water-plant. But a little observation will suggest that these seed-pods behave very strangely, for every few seconds they are subject to vigorous, convulsive movements as if they were in a strong current, although the water of the pool is sure to be still. The tube, being so flexible, bends with every movement of the grub inside, and these spasms are caused by its undulating its body to keep up a circulation of water through the tube and supply the gills with oxygen. They may also be seen punting themselves freely across the tiny patches of open water between the

CASE-BEARING MIDGE LARVA

weed-masses, propelled by some unseen force which is very puzzling until the appearance of a snake-like head, which is darted out from either end of the tube as its owner takes its bearings for the steering of this curious craft. Sometimes the tube will get lodged, and then it rocks with agitation, and the slim head shoots out first from one end and then the other, so rapidly that one could easily imagine a two-headed creature lived inside. Finally the reason of the obstruction is discovered, the sharp jaws loosen the boat from the obstacle, and peace is restored. The tube is lined with silk, and can be moored by threads of the same material when the owner wishes to be stationary, and the entrances are closed with silk, as are Caddis-worm cases, when the grub is about to pupate.

There is a peculiar group of moths whose caterpillars form cases very similar to those of Caddis-worms ; they feed upon the leaves of trees, shifting their tube as they require

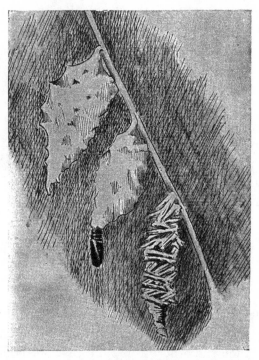

CASES OF PSYCHE

fresh feeding-grounds. These are the basket insects, or bag-worms.

When the caterpillar first hatches from the egg it binds itself to a leaf with a loop of silk and proceeds to build the case on to this first strand. In some tropical species these cases may attain a fair size, and give the trees a very strange

158

appearance. They are destructive caterpillars, and may strip trees entirely of their foliage over a considerable stretch of ground. Some species decorate their cases with small twigs ; in others one end tapers to a slender tip ; others are very like cigarettes. Our only British representatives of this family are very minute, and build little tents rather like the caps which fall off buds as they open. As the caterpillar grows the case is enlarged, but it does not quit its home for pupation. Indeed, only the males leave the home case when they finally emerge with wings ; the female is wingless, and she lives and dies in the case. After she has laid her eggs and wrapped each one up carefully in fluff, which comes from the tip of her

HOUSE OF SHEATH-MAKER
Hugh Main

body, she dies in a far corner of the tube, where she will not get in the way of the hatching of the eggs. It is thought that the little caterpillars directly they hatch out feed on the dead body of their mother, but until this is definitely proved we will try not to believe that they are capable of such an act of barbarity.

159

CHAPTER XIII

INSECTS WHICH SHOW LIGHTS

THERE is no doubt that insects which are active in the daytime are guided a great deal in finding one another by colour and pattern. But many insects are resting during the day and only come out in the twilight or in the dark, when their working day really begins ; of course, colour and form are of no use to these nocturnal insects, for they cannot see in the dark, and must depend upon some other sense than sight in order to find their food or their mates. There are some moths whose wings are of a pure silvery white, and some of a light silvery grey ; these when they fly at twilight (such as the Ghost Swifts) seem to catch every glimmer of light, and are quite easily seen as they flit about against a dark background ; but other moths which do not come out in ballroom attire, but on the contrary have their wings modestly patterned in greys and browns (usually streaked and blotched to make them still more indefinite), would not be visible at all in a diffused light. So we find that there are numbers of insects which have had to evolve special methods of finding one another because their eyesight is no help to them however well developed it may be.

The sense which guides many of them is the sense of smell. In the pairing season (as was described in Chapter VII) some moths put out scent on little plumed brushes which is so strong that the males—whose sense of smell is formed to catch that particular scent—can perceive it from a very long distance. Most of us have tested the fact in this country with females of the Oak-egger and the Emperor Moth and Vapourers. All the males in the neighbourhood will collect and flutter round the place where the female is confined, and even if the female moth herself is taken away they will continue to visit the box or cage she was in for a long period afterward, as long, in fact, as the scent is perceptible.

There are insects which depend upon the sense of hearing. The cricket's chirping at dusk and the ticking of the Death Watch are love-songs of the males, and there are other sounds produced by the male which act upon the special sense-organs possessed by the female for recording that sound.

A certain group of night-flying beetles have evolved a signalling system of their own for the very same purpose, which they carry out in the hours of darkness by means of specially developed organs. These are the fireflies, glow-worms, and glow-beetles or Luminous Click-beetles.

This power of illuminating is possessed by beetles belonging to two separate families. Nearly all those belonging to the firefly family (*Lampyridæ*), in which are included our British glow-worms, have this power, and some members of the very large family of Click-beetles (*Elateridæ*). The position of the light-organs on the body of light-giving beetles varies in the different genera. Among glow-worms it is the wingless female only which shows a light, and by this means is made visible to her mate flying above her while she crawls about in the grass and low herbage. There is a faint glow on the male and on the larvæ and eggs too, but the female

THE FEMALE OAK-EGGER
Hugh Main

has a real organ for emitting light, and we have added proof that the use of the light is to attract the males in the fact that he has large, well-developed eyes, while in the female the eyes are small and not more developed when she is mature than when she is a larva.

Among the Luminous Click-beetles of tropical countries light-organs are carried by both males and females, and it is interesting to note that the eyes are equally developed in both sexes.

Some of the largest of the glow-beetles have two sets of lights ; one set on the body under the wing-cases, where it is only visible while the insect is flying, and a pair of large, round light-organs on the thorax, which when lighted look like two fiery eyes. Their shape and position suggests that they are some sort of protection to these beetles ; for instance, if a bird were to peck at one of the glow-beetles and it switched on the lights in these enormous eyes in all probability the bird would leave it alone.

GLOW-BEETLE FROM SOUTH AMERICA

It is fascinating to learn the system by which the beetle produces its own light. To understand it clearly it is best to study in detail the light-organs of the large glow-beetle, which lives on sugar-cane, because those organs have been studied recently and many experiments carried out in connexion with them.

It was thought at one time that the light of all fireflies was phosphorescent—that is, that it was caused by some sort of material in the beetle's body which absorbed rays of light and gave them out again in darkness, as is done by luminous paint. But firefly light is far more interesting than this, for it is

163

actually caused by combustion ; this means that there is a certain material manufactured by the beetle which is burnt when it comes in contact with oxygen. Floating about in the body-fluid of insects are tiny drops of fat which act as a sort of reserve store. Some of these fat-bodies, as they are called, are collected to form a layer of cells in the light-organ, together with cells of another substance which is also present

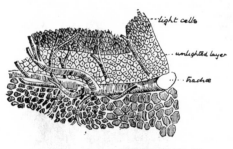

SECTION OF THE LIGHT-ORGAN OF
A GLOW-BEETLE

in other parts of the beetle's body and aids in digesting its food. These two substances together make the material which lights up. The third factor for producing the light—oxygen—is also near at hand. We know that every insect is supplied with oxygen, which is carried by fine branched tubes all over the body. Those that pass through the light-organs are extremely delicate, and so thinly covered at the tips that when muscles press upon the tubes the air is forced out and the oxygen comes in contact with the special cells, causing them to ignite or illumine. As fast as the material is used up the supply is renewed, however long the lights are kept burning.

Now it has been proved by experiments carried out in the laboratory that the light is increased by adding more oxygen up to a certain degree ; it can be further intensified by raising the temperature, but here again a maximum is reached, after which, if the temperature is raised still higher, the light decreases. This is because the heat produces a change in the nature of the fat-bodies. In the natural state the insect would raise its own body temperature by getting excited either by the presence of enemies or of other beetles, and perhaps too by the mere working of its muscles.

Now all this, although very wonderful, would be of no manner of use to the beetle if it took place inside its horny skin, any more than a lantern would be useful if it were made entirely of a material through which the light could not pass. But as in a lantern one side is transparent, so in the tough skin of the beetle

FEMALE GLOW-WORM SENDING FORTH HER LIGHT SIGNAL
Hugh Main

the layers just over the light-organs have hardly any chitin between them, and the light shines through. And in addition to this there is a reflector: a layer of cells of tiny crystals which reflect the rays of light and intensify their brilliancy.

Thus our glow-beetle has a perfect and complete lighting outfit, consisting of a lantern with one window and a reflector, a luminant for the lantern, and a means of igniting the luminant. When the light of these organs is suddenly flashed on it becomes visible to us, because the beetle has added oxygen to the light-cells, and when this grows brighter it is because the temperature of the beetle's body is rising.

The light that is produced is very powerful and will shine through quite thick substances. An American naturalist who was observing wild life in the jungles of Guiana described how he tried without success to smother it. Once, when he was watching for some of the night-prowling creatures, he happened to notice crawling near him a large glow-beetle which was such a good specimen that he picked it up and put it in his pocket.

MALE GLOW-WORM
Hugh Main

In a little while there was such a glow shining through the cloth that he took it out and wrapped it in his mackintosh. The light shone through more brilliantly than before; no doubt the beetle was getting excited by that time at finding itself imprisoned. He then wrapped it first in brown paper and afterward in his mackintosh, but even then the light was so strong that he was forced to let the beetle go, though very reluctantly, for it was such a good specimen. But it would

MALE GLOW-WORM, HEAD RETRACTED, SHOWING UNDER-SIDE
Hugh Main

have been useless to try to hide himself while he carried such a powerful pocket lantern.

Another amusing story is that of a naturalist in Cuba who picked up what he thought must be a luminous frog. He was not particularly learned in reptiles, and could not recollect ever having heard of such a thing, but carried it carefully home, thinking it must be a new species. However, when he examined it in his laboratory it turned out to be no unusual specimen, but it had evidently been dining very sumptuously off fireflies, and the light from these was shining through its body.

Some of the Canadian fireflies have been seen actually to signal to one another. Of course, there is no code adopted by them, but the male flashed its light on and off as it flew around, and the female gave an answering flash from the grasses where she had settled, and so guided the male to the spot. These beetles were tested by an electric lamp with a light as near an imitation of the firefly's own as could be produced; the experiment was very successful, for both male and female were made to flash their lights in response to it.

CHAPTER XIV

MUSICAL INSTRUMENTS

FOR want of a better expression we may say musical instruments, although in most instances the sound which is produced can scarcely be classed as music. They are really the special organs of insects which are designed to cause some sort of vibration of the air. As a rule these sounds are a means of communication between the male and the female ; those which we know so well, such as the chirping of grasshoppers or the humming of gnats, are made by the male insect only, and usually the female only possesses an organ for catching the sounds which he makes, but in some groups both sexes possess organs of hearing.

Some of the sounds made by insects are very loud, others are soft ; some are pleasant to our ears, others distinctly the reverse. There are many which we cannot describe, because we do not hear them ; we only know by seeing a vibration of some part of the insect's body that some sound is being produced. It is therefore quite reasonable to suppose that many sounds produced by insects are quite unknown to us. We have no clue if the organ producing them does not happen to be visible to us and a movement is not apparent. Anybody who has watched a short-horned grasshopper fiddling to his mate must have noticed also the attitude of strained attention on her part. Either she is listening very

168

hard, or else, as seems quite probable, she is emitting a little song in answer to her troubadour which we unfortunately are unable to appreciate, because it is produced by some invisible musical organ.

Very delightful is the humming of bees, perhaps because it is associated in our minds with warm summer days, clover fields, flowers, blue skies, and sunshine. It is a soothing sound of which one does not tire, and the rise and fall of the booming of a bumble-bee as it zigzags across a field has a charm all its own. This humming is produced by the air passing through the two pairs of wings, which are held in position horizontally by a mechanical contrivance that locks the fore-wings and hind-wings together very neatly. In some insects— Hover-flies and bluebottles, for example—the buzzing noise is caused by large open air-tubes, in which the air makes just such a booming as we can make for ourselves with a shell or any hollow object if we pass it rapidly through the air.

GRASSHOPPER
FIDDLING

The up and down motion of a butterfly's wings makes little sound. These are not locked tightly together, though in some species there is a little hook on one pair which fits into a groove in the other. The insect does not glide, but beats the air lightly ; we can only detect a soft rustling if the insect flies near us or if a number of them pass in a flock.

But the teasing, insistent note of a gnat is due to something quite different, being made by a very neat little musical organ on the wings. It consists of two movable bars at the base of the wings ; one bar has a ridge, and the other is furnished with teeth which move against the ridge while the insect is in flight.

Most of the squeaking, chirping, and fiddling of insects is accomplished by rubbing different parts of the wings, legs, or body against one another, and these parts have little knobs or various shaped projections for the production of different notes of sound.

Some members of the beaked insects group rub the

Scales (greatly enlarged)

DETAILS OF GNAT'S WING

first pair of legs against the beak. Among grass-hoppers some males of the long-horned species make an astoundingly loud chirping by drawing a file on the lower left wing against a knob on the upper right wing ; crickets also fiddle, but they rub the fore-wing against the hind one ; they do this at such an extraordinary rate that the wings show only a blurred out-line caused by the vibration. In the short-horned group the chirping is made by rubbing the hind-leg against the wing-cases. In all these it is only the male which makes the sound, so far as we know.

The vibration of the wings of the Death's-head Moth and Humming-bird Hawk Moth causes their musical humming. The sound made by the Death's-head Moth is supposed to resemble the peculiar humming of swarming bees so exactly that when the moth enters a hive to steal honey, as it is so fond of doing, the bees are said to allow it to steal without attempting to prevent it, because they get the idea that it

MALE FIELD CRICKET AT MOUTH OF BURROW
Hugh Main

must be one of themselves since it can reproduce a sound which they recognize. But this solution of the riddle needs more proof before it can be accepted. No really satisfactory reason has yet been put forward as to why some insects are able to get into these well-protected colonies and take advantage of them, while others are slain at once, without hesitation. The Death's-head Moth if handled can also squeak like a mouse or a bird ; on several occasions cats have been known to catch these moths and bring them into the house, and it is quite possible that they have been deceived by the sound, and think they have something good to eat. Needless to say, the owner of the cat rejoices thereat, because Death's-head Moths are not easy to acquire. The sound is made by the moth rubbing the palps of its mouth against its proboscis. The caterpillar makes a similar sound, though not so loud. There is an Indian Hawk Moth the caterpillar of which makes a peculiar hissing which is quite alarming, especially as it rears itself at the same time into a terrifying attitude.

The ticking sound made by the Death Watch is not produced by a special organ, but is made by his tapping his horny head against some solid object. This beetle lives in burrows in old furniture or the wood of old buildings, in which its grub can do an immense amount of damage by riddling the solid beams with holes (as recently happened in the roof of Westminster Hall). The ticking which we hear is made by the male beetle serenading his lady-love, the sound produced being of a regular rhythm like the ticking of a watch.

A strange superstition has arisen among country folk that

when this sound is heard some member of the household will die—hence the name Death Watch Beetle. As this quaint serenading of the ladies is carried out during certain months of the year there ought to be a corresponding season for family deaths.

The drumming of the cicadas is an entirely different process to any of the foregoing, and the volume of sound which they produce is such that it can only be described by those who have actually heard it And as those who have heard it are quite at a loss to find words adequately to express the sound, the full realization of such a song—if it may rightly be called a song—must be left to

A BRITISH CICADA (NEW FOREST)
Hugh Main

individual experience. It has been variously compared to the whistle of a locomotive, a factory whistle, or a watchman's rattle. At certain seasons the cicadas drum all day in a wood, and the human ear is almost deafened by the loud, continuous throbbing vibration, as if all manner of machinery were going at the same time. The noise is extremely trying, and it is fortunate that it ceases at nightfall. In the case of this insect it is difficult to guess what prompts the male to keep up this continuous racket. It must be a source of enjoyment to himself, for the females are never observed near the males at such

173

times, nor has it been discovered that they possess any organ of hearing. The sound-producing organ of the cicada is under the body ; it consists of a pair of sacs, formed of skin, which fill with air and expel it by a contraction of the muscles. The visible outer parts of the organs are like parchment disks, and the sides are corrugated, so that they are very like a pair of little concertinas. The sound is produced by the air being forced out through two circular openings ; these may be partially closed by movements of the muscles, which has the effect of making this note increase or decrease in loudness, according to the size of the opening. By this means the cicada is able to throw his voice around like a ventriloquist, and it is most difficult to guess the distance from which the sound comes or to locate the insect.

We may sometimes be irritated by the sound of insects— by mosquitoes which haunt our bedroom at night, or the bluebottle which keeps us awake in the early hours of the morning—but if insects were silent we should certainly miss their tiny voices, and the beauty of the country is certainly enhanced, even if we do not altogether realize it, by the mingling of their various little notes and the rhythmic beating of their million tiny wings in the air.

CHAPTER XV

MOTHER INSECTS

IN the insect world the female is of far more importance than the male. He is generally an insignificant little thing ; he does not live as long as she does, and she is usually a great deal bigger than her spouse. Among some of the beetles, where the male has to fight for the female, such as Stag Beetles, the male is decidedly bigger, and is of a stronger build altogether. But this is quite an exception ; if there is any difference in size it is as a general rule the female which is larger.

The parent insects in no wise look after or protect their young, as do some of the higher animals. Most young insects are so entirely different from the parents that the latter would probably have to develop a special sense-organ in order to recognize them. But most of the young larvæ are very independent little creatures, fitted up by nature with all the simpler organs which are necessary to enable them to get along by themselves. All that is required of the parents is that the eggs should be placed so that they are not too accessible to enemies and not beyond easy reach of food for the larvæ. All this is carried out by the mother insect with minute care, and sometimes even with great personal risk to herself.

One fact which comes as a surprise the first time we learn

it is that in some groups of insects there are only females, these being so constructed that they are able to form the eggs and fertilize them in their own body.

Where insects require to vary their habits or form new instincts the male is necessary for the welfare of the species. One male will fertilize many females, and will not keep to members of the same brood ; therefore he will bring new elements to mix with the material which forms the egg ; this cannot take place when the female fertilizes her own eggs. The little larva which hatches out of an egg that is produced by the female of one brood and the male of another has probably a more elastic character, so that if necessary it can strike out on its own into some new variety of form. Let us suppose, for instance, that food is scarce and that a caterpillar must either form a taste for a new sort of food or starve. Many caterpillars do die when such an event happens, but perhaps one caterpillar out of a hundred will acquire this new taste ; and if this habit is inherited a new race may result.

MALE EMPEROR MOTH
Hugh Main

176

Among the higher types of insects we always find male and female differing from one another in well-defined characters ; it is among the insects which lead a humdrum existence.

FEMALE EMPEROR MOTH
Hugh Main

with very little variety in the way of events throughout their life-history, that there is sometimes this remarkable scarcity of males. Take the stick insects, for instance, among some species of which males are often very rare ; the females can produce eggs without them for an extraordinary number of generations. Stick insects hang among the foliage by day (without movement, lest the effect of their wonderful camouflage should be lost) and feed by night.

M

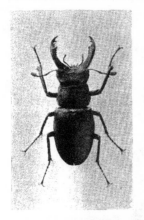

MALE STAG BEETLE
Hugh Main

They hardly move from the trees which they first climbed after hatching, unless the food-supply comes to an end. One would imagine they must quite enjoy the time of their moults as providing a little entertainment to while away the days ; and if an enemy raids them and gobbles up a few perhaps even that makes a welcome diversion in the awful monotony of their existence. They never even try to avoid an enemy except by walking away.

Stick insects do not seem to need special instincts to meet special emergencies in their lives as do most insects. Just a mechanical response to anything which affects their sense-organs is all that they need in the way of intelligence.

There is another group of insects among which males are rare, or quite unknown ; these are the Stem Saw-flies which lay their eggs on particular plants, in the stems of which the grubs live when they hatch. Here is another life-history which is singularly lacking in excitement. The chief feature of the sawfly is a truly wonderful little instrument, the saw, which the mother insect carries to make a little slit in the tissue of the stems of plants

FEMALE STAG BEETLE
Hugh Main

178

MALE AND FEMALE LEAF INSECT

H. Shirley

or between the tissue of leaves in which to place the eggs safely. All the sense that is required of the mother sawfly is to respond to the scent of the right kind of plant, which starts the whole complicated machinery for preparing a place and laying the eggs.

Compared with the romantic life-histories of some other insects that we know of, whose whole existence is made up of thrilling adventures, the life of these Stem Sawflies is very tame. It is not surprising that males are rare among them. Indeed, in many species the male is supposed not to exist at all; at any rate, he has never been seen. Though many thousands of insects have been bred out on purpose to settle this question they have always been females; and as some are very common species, it certainly is odd that the male insect, if it exists, should be unknown.

We have said that parent insects do not take care of their young, but the earwigs are a curious exception. The mother earwig makes a hole in the ground, and at the bottom hollows out a little nest in which the eggs are laid; and instead of leaving them to hatch she actually sits on them, and broods them as a hen does! No creature dares come near while this is taking place; the mother will defend her nest fiercely, curling her body over so as to threaten the enemy with her forceps. After the eggs are hatched the mother may still be found with her brood, guarding them, and collecting them under her for warmth, absurdly like a hen. Even when the mother is not with them the family is usually together, and may be found in little groups under stones, or soil, or bark.

180

Two distinct types of insect build very wonderful nests, the Praying Mantis and the Tortoise Beetle—insects belonging to very different orders; but, curiously enough, their

NEST OF PRAYING MANTIS

nests are very like one another in material and in the way they are put together, though in size, of course, they are very different, because Praying Mantises are mostly large insects, and all the Tortoise Beetles small.

181

The female mantis carries a useful collection of tools at the end of her body, and she uses each in turn when building her nest, which is a most fascinating operation to watch.

INTERIOR OF NEST OF PRAYING MANTIS

The nest is many times larger than the body of the mantis, which is surprising when it is realized that all the material of which it is composed comes out of her body. All the time she is building and using up the gummy fluid more material is being manufactured inside her body, and this supply is kept up until the nest is finished. Building is usually begun in the very early hours of the morning, and takes about an hour. The material comes out in fluid form, and is of two kinds, a gummy fluid which hardens very quickly into a sort of horn, very tough and strong, and a frothy fluid which turns into a sort of sponge ; this second material fills up all the chinks of the nest and probably keeps the eggs healthy, because it is full of air-bubbles. The mantis chooses a stem or a stone and builds on to this firm foundation, bringing out the gummy material, which she flattens into ribbons between two tiny plates ; when the strip of ribbon is long enough she cuts off a length by bringing the same little plates together at the tip and neatly pinching it off. The lengths are placed on the top of one another, and the eggs are pressed into the ribbon before it hardens ; this hardening is only a matter of a few seconds, so that the work must not pause or be interrupted. The eggs are set at equal distances apart by means of a pair of pointed organs ; these also manipulate the spongy matter after it has been beaten into a froth, like white of egg, by another pair of organs, which are spade-shaped and twirl round in the fluid so rapidly that their movement is almost invisible. This frothy mass is pressed round the eggs to make a padding for them : then another ribbon is put into the mass, with another row of little eggs ; and so the building proceeds until the whole cone-shaped nest is completed and covered over with a coating of gummy varnish.

It is a wonderful piece of work, so fashioned that the eggs are as safe as they can be made, protected from cold, damp, and enemies, yet with little passages inside for the young mantises to creep out by directly they hatch.

Some of the mother insects possess special instruments

(ovipositors) for placing the eggs in the most favourable position ; these are of a great variety of design. Some are simple tubes through which the eggs pass by the working of strong muscles. Among grasshoppers this tube is curved and has a sharp tip, which is driven into the soil or a crack in the bark or rotten wood or wherever the species places the eggs. When the eggs are laid in trees the mother has to

A FEMALE GRASSHOPPER LAYING EGGS IN THE GROUND

take a curious angle against the bark, for the ovipositor is usually long and none too easy to manage. When the tip has been brought up against the trunk the insect drives it in by working it to and fro until it is through the bark; then the eggs are squeezed out of the end of the tube, and the hole generally filled up with a gummy fluid which shuts out enemies and through which the young grasshoppers must gnaw a way when they hatch.

These eggs are not laid very far in the bark, but merely in cracks. The grubs of some insects, however, live in burrows right inside and feed on the wood itself; the mothers of these grubs must place the eggs far enough in for the grubs to start their burrowing at once when they hatch ; therefore their ovipositors must be slender and yet strong.

The Fir Borer or Wood Wasp is one of these insects ; the female may be seen on hot days in summer in any of our woods where there are larches, flying rather slowly, with her long and bright ovipositor stretched stiff out behind. This

Borer is large, and coloured brown and yellow ; it is popularly taken for a hornet or a wasp and treated with great respect by the country people, who imagine the ovipositor to be a sting.

Young trees are not chosen to lay the eggs in because the wood is too hard, but felled logs answer the purpose—or if timber is inclined to be diseased the mother Borer soon finds it out. As the grubs take two or three years to become mature it frequently happens that timber in which grubs are hatched is used for building outhouses, or even dwellings, without disturbing the insects inside.

WOOD WASP
Hugh Main

Then one summer the nerves of the human inhabitants suffer many shocks as these big inoffensive insects, whose appearance is so very alarming, suddenly begin to emerge from the timber in numbers.

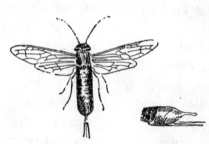

WOOD WASP, OR GIANT BORER

Quite the most wonderful ovipositor possessed by mother insects is that of large insects of the group called parasitic wasps, whose grubs prey on the grubs of these Borers. The largest we have in England is named Rhyssa.

It is probably when the Borer grubs have hatched out and begun to feed that the eggs of this parasite are laid, because the Rhyssa grubs cannot gnaw a passage through the wood as the Borer grubs do. Their mouth is only a sharp-pointed beak formed for piercing the skin of grubs and sucking out the soft parts of their body. Nobody can be quite certain what is taking place inside a tree-trunk, and to reach the burrows the ovipositor has to be very long indeed, and yet slender so as to push its way between the fibres of wood.

The mother Rhyssa then has need of very highly developed instincts to master the problems connected with her egg-laying. From outside the trunk she has to judge the best point to insert her ovipositor in order to strike into a burrow ; if she makes a mistake the little Rhyssa larva must die. She has also to be very careful in manipulating her delicate ovipositor, which is very much longer and finer than that of Borers ; if it gets fixed in the wood then she must die.

This is how the task is accomplished according to the descriptions of several people who have watched the Rhyssa at work.

The insect first walks about on the trunk, searching for a good place to begin, stopping every now and then to touch the bark with her antennæ. It is argued that she probably finds the same hole that the Borer used for laying her eggs, but it is quite likely that the Rhyssa can feel the vibration of the wood from the Borer grubs' jaws as they gnaw it below.

Her antennæ are very delicate and sensitive, and can quite well inform her of movements and thrills which would not be perceived by human beings. Having decided upon the

exact spot, the ovipositor at the end of the body is raised
until the tip rests against the bark, but in a slanting position
which would be of no use for drilling a hole. The ovipositor,
being of such extraordinary length compared with the rest

RHYSSA GRUB (LEFT) AND FIR-BORER GRUB (RIGHT) IN THEIR
BURROWS INSIDE A TREE-TRUNK

of the insect, cannot be held upright, but the Rhyssa has a
method of getting it into position without any risk of snap-
ping the delicate tip. She proceeds without waste of time
to *shorten* it by drawing it into her body, where the base of it
curls up like a watch-spring inside a skin sac formed for that
very purpose. When the ovipositor is shortened sufficiently
for it to take an upright position against the bark the protecting sheath is parted and held on each side, and boring begins.

187

The insect now has got it under control, and can bear upon it while she drills by twisting it to and fro with the help of very strong muscles at its base in her body. Then when it has reached one of the burrows inside the tree the tip of the ovipositor opens and lets out the eggs. The drilling occupies some time, as one would suppose, and while it is in progress the mother Rhyssa runs great risks. Any insect-eating bird which is hunting near could hardly miss such a tit-bit, and she is quite helpless, because the withdrawing of the ovipositor is a still more delicate operation than the boring on account of notches near the tip, which would be liable to catch if there were any sudden movement. Altogether it is a most perilous and marvellous feat which this mother insect performs in order to place her eggs in a suitable position for the larvæ to get their natural food.

Another type of mother is the female Tsetse Fly. This is a highly developed form of fly which carries the egg and hatches it inside her body, feeding it by means of special glands which are called milk-glands. Only one larva at a time is brought up in this way, and when it is ready to pupate the mother places it in a suitable spot; this must be shady and near water, and the soil must be loose so that it can burrow down at once. In tropical Africa, where this fly is found, the soil which is least likely to be hard and dry is gravel; and this is precisely the sort of soil the Tsetse Fly

PUPARIA OF TSETSE FLY
Hugh Main

188

chooses—rough, coarse, sandy gravel, into which the grub wriggles at once and pupates. The mother insect may fly miles in search of such a locality. But perhaps all this would never have been found out if scientists had not interested themselves in the life-history of the fly in order to destroy it if possible and check the awful disease the germs of which it carries. Knowledge of its habits has given very good results. A great deal of trouble was taken, a great deal of money was spent, and those men working in the sleeping sickness district carried their lives in their hands, for they were always in danger of contracting the disease.

But now a trick is played on the flies ; artificial breeding-grounds were arranged which should have everything the grubs required. The mother flies soon found them out, and came in numbers to put their grubs into the rough, loose soil under canopies of branches which kind men planned for them. They do not know, of course, that these same kind men send round natives to these pupating grounds to collect all the pupæ and destroy them before they shall hatch out. One man will collect as many as three hundred in a few hours, and that makes a real difference to the number of flies in that part of the country. All round the Victoria Nyanza in Uganda quite a lot of clearing has been done in this way, and the flies have decreased in numbers enormously.

CHAPTER XVI

INSECTS AND FLOWERS

INSECTS and flowers are so associated in our minds that we can scarcely think of one without the other. Throughout the months when insects are most active flowers are most numerous, and in winter, when insects are either dead or asleep, there are no flowers to be seen either.

With the first warm days of spring, when we see hive-bees and bumble-bees venturing out of their winter quarters, we find the first wild flowers, dandelions, celandine, and willow catkins. And in late autumn if we notice a few belated blackberry-blossoms in sheltered nooks we shall probably see some sleepy specimens of brightly marked Hover-flies feeding on them.

The relationship between flowers and insects is of a very close nature, and so necessary is each to the other that if there were no insects many species of plants would die out, and if for even a year there were no flowers then many species of insects would cease to exist.

We must first consider why flowers should encourage insects to visit them. A flower, in order to ripen its seeds, has by some means to convey pollen—the golden dust which develops in the centre of a flower-head—to that part of it which is called the stigma. Various flowers have various shaped stigmas, but they nearly all have a sticky surface,

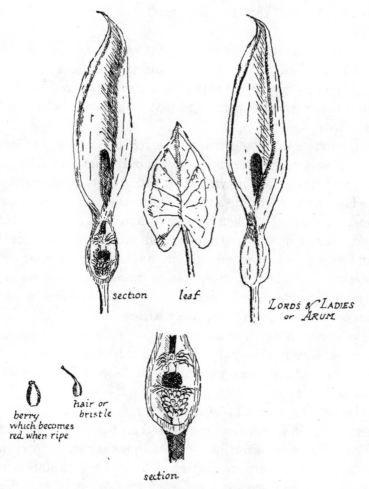

section   leaf

LORDS & LADIES
or ARUM

berry
which becomes
red when ripe

hair or
bristle

section

HOW FLOWERS ARE FERTILIZED
Peter Scott

so that the pollen will be held when once it is scattered
over them. The scattering of this pollen, then, is the

191

problem ; after that has happened the flower can do the rest.

Some kinds of plants fertilize themselves by bending the heads of pollen, when it is ripe, until they touch the stigma. But it is always an advantage if the seeds are fertilized by pollen from another plant—crossed with another plant, as it is called.

In some species the flowers are fertilized by wind ; but the wind is very wasteful, and often only a small quantity of the pollen which is blown away is taken to its destination.

The surest method, and therefore the most satisfactory one, is to have the pollen personally conveyed to other plants and rubbed on to the stigmas, and this delicate mission is undertaken and carried out by insects who collect the precious dust and distribute it by means of a special air-service, thus — all unconsciously of course — filling a very important post in the scheme of nature.

We see, then, that insects are very necessary to some flowers, but it does not appear equally evident until we look into the subject carefully that flowers are necessary to insects.

During the course of ages, however, flowers have not only held out bribes and allurements to tempt insects to perform the kindly office of fertilizing them, but they have provided them with the very necessities of life. Large numbers of insects live on honey and pollen ; some depend on flowers for temporary shelter ; and some make use of them as breeding-places for the next generation.

When flowers first appeared on the globe insects began to develop many different forms. The first flowers were prob-
192

ably self-fertilized or wind-fertilized. It would be interesting to know exactly the form of the first flower which relied on insects to propagate it, and also the exact form of the first insect to take up this duty. We can only guess at either.

CAMBERWELL BEAUTY DRINKING NECTAR
H. Shirley

But it is quite certain that with the commencement of that mutual service an endless variety of forms both of flowers and of insects must have been started. For as flowers developed different designs to meet the requirements of insects, to attract, compel, guide, and organize their visits, insects on their part evolved special organs to carry out their responsibilities in the partnership in the most effective manner.

This has resulted in certain flowers being visited only by

N

special insects, because the structure of the flower is such that every other visitor but the privileged ones is shut out. And these certain insects are privileged because they are of the precise form to serve the plant in the best manner.

Bees and butterflies have special mouths for feeding on

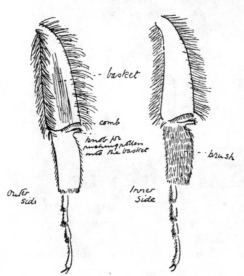
nectar. There are bees with short tongues to lap it out of those flowers which have placed it within easy reach for them. And there are bees with long tongues and butterflies and moths with a slender, long proboscis to lap or suck the honey which is contained in some flowers with tube-shaped throats.

HIND-LEG OF A BUMBLE-BEE

The wonder of this relationship between insects and flowers is that those that have developed special mouth-parts for obtaining nectar from special blossoms are just those particular forms of insects which can fertilize those blossoms and no others.

So when we see a big bumble-bee pushing aside the flaps which guard the nectar-store of a bean-blossom we know that her furry coat will brush off the pollen as she crawls inside to get at the nectar and that some of the pollen will come off on the stigma of the next flower she visits. The

194

bean-flower keeps its flaps so tightly closed that only a strong insect can force its way in. If little beetles or flies were allowed to creep through they would take honey, but would not be able to carry any pollen away with them, because they are too small.

Flowers have to tempt the right sort of insect to visit them, and yet keep out all the undesirables. And this they manage to do by such ingenious methods that it is quite difficult not to regard them as reasonable beings — and extra clever reasonable beings — who just sit down and think out what will be the best

BUMBLE-BEE COLLECTING POLLEN
H. Shirley

scheme to make insects carry out their wishes in precisely the right way.

Of course, flowers offer liberal wages. It would be useless to expect insects to take so much trouble for a poor return.

Hive-bees and bumble-bees can collect so much nectar from flowers that they are able to store it ; and some flowers that are without nectar have a sweet juice in their tissues which provides good meals for a visitor. Then pollen is very generously provided for the beetles and flies and thrips that live on it. It is the good policy of the kinds of flowers on which these insects feed to spread out far more pollen than they could possibly eat. So we see the open kind of flower—daisies, sunflowers, and the like—with tiny florets, brimming with pollen like golden goblets of wine, crowded together in the centre of the disk so thickly that no insects can feed there without knocking against neighbouring florets, and so getting pollen on some part of the body, usually on hairs and spines. This is exactly what will benefit the flower. We see the little beetles and flies fairly wallowing in pollen while they feed,

ROSECHAFER FEEDING ON POLLEN

and they fly away flecked with gold dust, some of which is sure to be appropriated by the next flower which provides a meal.

Watch bumble-bees and hive-bees on a sunflower's yellow disk. Part of their duty is to collect pollen to make into bee-bread for the young bees. As they crawl about the hairs and spines of their body and legs will become smothered with pollen. This they collect by combing it out with the spines on the inner side of their legs, designed for that very purpose, and ramming it down into little baskets which they carry on their hind pair. But not all of it can be collected; enough is left entangled in their hair to fertilize the next sunflower-head they visit. The ray of larger florets round the disks of these flowers have no pollen; they are only to attract attention, like a circle of little flags hung out to advertise the goods.

We have only so far been considering the *food* offered by flowers to insects, but there are cases where the flower supplies a breeding-place; and here the mother insect does all the work, the fetching and carrying of the pollen, not for herself, but in return for food for her caterpillars when they hatch.

There is a most curious and interesting example of this in connexion with plants called yucca, which have large, bell-shaped flowers fertilized by the Yucca Moth, a pretty little moth with cream-coloured wings that have a burnished appearance.

The flowers are ready to be visited exactly at the season when the Yucca Moth is ready to lay its eggs, and as they are open for one night only all the business has to be done quickly or not at all. The mother moth creeps into the big bell-flower and collects some pollen, which she rolls into a ball and carries under a pair of palpi below her pro-

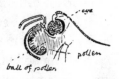

HEAD OF YUCCA MOTH

boscis. The palpi are of a special shape on purpose for this work. They are much larger than is usual among moths, and have on the inner surface a row of strong spines which serve to keep the ball of pollen in position. Next the moth makes for the flower's pistil, and piercing it with her ovipositor lays her eggs in it.

Below the pistil is the little chamber which later will, if the flower is fertilized, contain seeds; by the time they have developed the little caterpillars will be hatched out, and these young seeds are what they require as food. Near by is a little funnel intended to receive pollen, and this the moth proceeds to stuff with the pollen she has been carrying. If this were not done no seeds would develop, so that she is really providing for her own brood, but, on the other hand, if it were not for her visit the flower would not be fertilized, so she is serving the plant at the same time.

If the caterpillars devoured all the seeds of course the yucca plant would be the loser, but so many seeds develop that the caterpillars cannot possibly eat more than two-thirds of the number before going down to the soil to pupate. And enough seeds remain to carry on the next generation of plants.

Another very remarkable case of mutual help is that of the fig, which is fertilized by tiny insects of the wasp order called fig insects. There are many species of these, which fertilize the flowers of different kinds of fig-trees.

What we call the seeds inside a fig are really florets growing inwardly to the centre. There are three kinds of florets, the males, bearing pollen, the females, and special florets in which the fig insects pass the greater part of their lives, only leaving them at the end of their existence so that the female fig insects may lay their eggs in another flower. As the insects push their way through the florets on their way out they get covered with pollen, and this the female carries to another flower when she creeps inside to lay her eggs.

Thus food and lodging are provided for the fig insects nearly all their lives in return for a few seconds' work, but only insects of that small size could accomplish it, and without that work the fig seeds would come to nothing.

There are other flowers which provide a temporary night's lodging to insects. These are flowers which close at night, such as poppies, anemones, daisies, etc. ; not only are the insects sheltered from damp, but it has been found that the temperature inside is actually higher than outside. So the insects are tempted to creep into such warm, dry quarters, and in return they carry off some pollen when they are released in the morning.

There are some flowers which actually make prisoners of their guests, and will not let them go until they have accomplished their task. Some of these lock-up flowers are the arums, whose pollen is found inside the bulb-shaped base of the spathe.

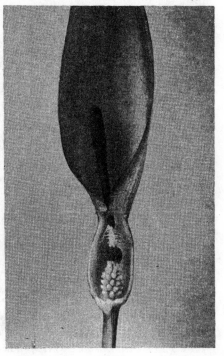

ARUM
Hugh Main

Two thick belts of stiff bristles guard the golden dust, one at the entrance to the bulb and a second ring farther down.

Arums have no nectar ; they have instead what we should consider a horrible smell, but this attracts insects that feed on dead animals and such things. The smell of nectar would not tempt such insects, but the very nasty arum scent is

199

alluring enough to tempt little flies and beetles to creep between the two barriers of curved spines until they reach the bottom. This is where the pollen is ripe for transporting. When once they are inside they are prisoners. At first they crawl round to explore, but there is no escape, because the bristles are so formed that they cannot be pushed aside from below. Finally the insects, in a panic, fly about, knocking against the male flowers and getting covered in pollen. Then a marvellous thing happens. The scattering of the pollen is the magic key to unlock their prison door, for at once the bristles begin to grow limp, and as they

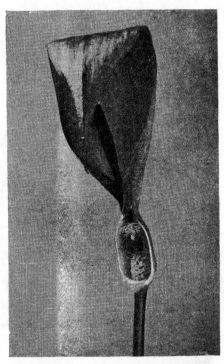

ARUM WHICH HAS BEEN POLLINATED, SHOW-
ING THE RING OF SPIKES DROOPING

Hugh Main

droop the insects find crevices between them through which they escape into the next chamber higher up. Here they find the female flowers and another belt of bristles above them. They rub against the female flowers and plaster their sticky stigmas with the pollen from their bodies ; this causes the second belt of bristles to droop, and so they creep through this

barrier too and are free.   Only by frightening their prisoners
and raising a cloud of pollen can the arums accomplish their
aim.   We can see this curious event taking place if we examine
the wild arums of our hedge-sides, the so-called lords-and-
ladies.   If we cut open the base of the spathe at the right
time, when the pollen is ripe, there we shall probably find a
crowd of little flies and beetles waiting for release.

Flowers which are visited by insects that fly by night keep
themselves for those privileged guests alone.

CHAPTER XVII

INSECTS WHICH MAKE MARKETABLE GOODS

SILKWORMS

ALL the pure silk that is used in making material is made by caterpillars commonly known as silkworms. A great number of insects spin silk—as also do spiders—but none of it equals that of the silkworm, for it is fine and yet strong, and has that particular shine which helps to give such good colours when silk is dyed. It is wonderful the different kinds of material which can be made of silk, from the flimsiest of gauzes to heavy, thick plush and velvet.

The silk that spiders make their webs of is very strong, and a cloth has been spun of it, but it is not glossy, and, besides, it is very difficult to collect enough of it to be of any use. In the course of ages silkworms have increased the amount of silk they produce, and being easy to rear and to breed, they have become domesticated by mankind, just as poultry, or cattle, or bees have been.

There are three distinct groups of silkworms, belonging to three families of moths. First there is the common white silkworm (*Bombyx mori*), used wherever silk is produced, in China, and Japan, and South Europe, as well as in other countries in which it has been introduced ; secondly there are the caterpillars of the handsome Wild Silk Moths (*Saturnidæ*), some of which are largely cultivated, though not to

202

anything like the extent of the *Bombyx mori* ; and thirdly there is an interesting group of African silkworms (*Anaphe*), which live in colonies and spin all their cocoons together in a mass, with an outer cover to protect it. These belong to the *Notodontidæ*, and though their silk is not of first-rate quality we will consider them later on.

Nobody really knows how long ago it was that the Eastern peoples discovered what useful material could be made out of the little yellow cocoons which *Bombyx mori* makes before turning into a moth. The first person we hear of in connexion with it is a Chinese empress named Si-ling, wife of a rather famous emperor, Huang-ki, who lived 2640 years before Christ. She encouraged her people to take up silk-culture, and in-terested herself in the growing

TAU SILK MOTH

of mulberry-trees, the tending of the silkworms, and the reeling and the weaving of the silk, which is still called *Si* in China. In those days it was chiefly the thin silk gauze that was made.

As not very much material was produced it was of course very expensive, and only royal families and grandees could afford to have their garments made of silk. The people of China kept the trade to themselves, and would not let the worms go out of the country for a long time. It is related that they were introduced into India by a Chinese princess who married an Indian prince, and carried eggs of *Bombyx mori* and some seeds of the mulberry-tree wrapped up in her head-dress, and so smuggled them out of the country to the new country she had adopted. It is a pretty little story, but not at all likely to be true. That silk was introduced into India is certainly true, but as it first appeared in North India it was in all probability brought there by merchants who would travel from China by the ordinary trade-routes.

When silk was finally taken up by the West the industry was much developed. Of course the Europeans would not be satisfied with the slow methods of working it by hand; they soon invented machines to do the reeling, twisting, and weaving; greater quantities of the raw silk could be made into material, and also the manufactured cloth was better, the thread more uniform, and the weaving more even when done by machinery.

There is another use for silkworms, discovered by the natives of Manchuria. They found that if the worm when it was full-fed was plunged into boiling water the silk could be pulled out of it in a thick, solid thread, which made excellent fish-lines. During the recent war this silk gut, as it is called, was used very extensively for sewing up wounds, as it was found to answer the purpose better than catgut. *Bombyx mori*, as a general rule, has only one generation a year, but of course it is of great advantage to rearers to have more, so those (bivoltine) which produce two are cultivated, and there are also other races which produce more than two (multivoltine).

The Japanese have methods of making the worms hatch

soon after the eggs are laid. This must take place within a few days, before they change colour from yellow to mauve ; when once the colour is altered they must go through a certain period of rest. The ingenious method is to set up an electric current by brushing the eggs several times a day with a feather brush. This can only be done in a hot, dry atmosphere, such as one gets in Oriental countries. Another means is to put the eggs alternately in hot water of a certain temperature and then in cold.

The rearing of silkworms is best carried out at a not very high temperature ; the worms will be slower in developing, but will be vigorous, and spin large cocoons. They cannot stand too much heat, and are always specially liable to disease if their quarters are not airy. Strong light should also be avoided, and the effect of moisture, either in the atmosphere or in their food, is sure to be fatal. It is possible to rear them on lettuce if the leaves are partly dried before being given to them, but experiments show that they take exactly double the time to develop. The right food is mulberry-leaves. In European silk-producing countries the white-berried mulberry (*Morus alba*) is always grown for them, it having been found that this suits them best, but there are many kinds of mulberry, and nearly all of them are used in other parts of the globe where silkworms are reared. Where a large number are reared trays are used which are arranged one above the other, allowing plenty of air to pass through, but not a draught. As the worms finish up their food paper sheets are put over them, with holes punctured in them, and the worms get through the holes after the fresh leaves, which are placed on the top of the sheets. Then the old leaves and the dirt can be taken away ; when the worms are small it would take very long, and would not be good for them, to remove them in any other way.

As the silkworms grow the sheets of paper are replaced by

RAGWORT SILK MOTH
H. Shirley

others with larger holes; and finally, when the time comes for spinning, twigs are given them to climb on. Heather is excellent for this, and looks very beautiful with golden cocoons against the dark green of its foliage.

The Chinese are superstitious regarding the welfare of the silkworm, and make very elaborate rules in the rearing-houses, which the workers have to observe to ensure the production of the best silk. A lady travelling in a country district of

whose microscopic seeds or spores escape through the skin of the worm and float about in the air. This explains why all the silkworms in a certain area used to catch the disease. But by destroying the sick worms before the spores ripen, and destroying all the eggs which are thought to be infected, the disease can be checked ; and it is very long now since there was an epidemic of muscardine. *Grasserie* is also a deadly malady which causes the worms to swell up and die ; it is started by cold and damp.

All these diseases have been investigated now by clever scientists ; the cause of them is known, and they may be prevented. This is a great advantage to people who depend upon the health of their silkworms for their living. But country people who go in for rearing are often very care-less, and the breeding-houses have to be visited by qualified inspectors to see that the silkworm diseases do not break out, or, if they have started, are checked.

The caterpillars of some of the beautiful moths called the Wild Silk Moths make very good silk, the best known being the Shantung silk or Tussore (spelt also Tasar and Tassar). The Tasar Moth reared in China is *Attacus pernyi*, a different species from the Indian one, *Attacus paphia*, but resembling it very much in appearance—the Chinese being the larger moth. The Indian Tasar spins a very hard, rounded cocoon, with a long stalk attached to a twig. The moths hatch out just after the monsoon, when the rains have helped to soften the cocoons. The silk of the Eri Moth is of a beautiful colour, being of a soft greenish brown; not much is produced, so that it is never seen in European shops, though it is worn much by Indians. Both Eri and Muga silk are produced in

India, but the latter chiefly in Assam. There the natives rear, spin, and weave it in their own homes, for their own use. The work is done chiefly by women and children.

ERI SILKWORM

The Wild Silk Moths are a very large family, and include some of the largest and most lovely moths. The delicate Moon Moth is of a wonderful green, and when settled among pale green leaves is very difficult to distinguish. There are two long tails to the wings which are very fragile. The moth seems often to injure them. The Moon Moth of

210

India is perhaps more beautiful than the one found in North America, though both are very beautiful. Another delicate species is *Grællsia Isabellæ*, which is found in South Europe, where the caterpillar feeds on the marine pine. The largest of the group and the largest known moth in the world is the

ERI SILK MOTH

Giant Atlas, found in the forest country of India; sometimes the wings measure fourteen inches across.

None of these moths feed either by sucking or biting, and one would think it quite impossible that they should ever emerge from the cocoon, which has often a gummy envelope to make it doubly safe. But in the first place the caterpillar in spinning up leaves the end near the head looser than the rest of the cocoon (it is easy to discover at which end the moth is going to emerge by examining a cocoon, and as it likes to crawl upward it is better to place the cocoon with the loose end uppermost), and secondly the moth is provided with special juices for softening the silk, so she not only pushes her soft head, through the loosely woven end, but with the juices of her mouth dissolves the strands of silk. Examine the cocoon from which a silk moth has emerged, and you will find the silk cut very neatly, as if with a tool. For this reason cocoons which are used for reeling must not be those from which moths have emerged, for it would be impossible to use up the short lengths with any success. The moths have to be killed inside the cocoon, and the thread reeled off entire.

The Anaphe silk of Africa is strong and useful, but is not regarded as ranking with the first-class silks. It is obtained from the strong, gummy envelope which surrounds a whole colony of cocoons spun up in a mass. The silkworms live in a family web spun up in the branch of a tree, leaving it in order to feed and returning to it at night. As they grow they spin larger webs and desert the old one, and finally at the end of their caterpillar days they spin the very tough outer cover (called parchment by the silk manufacturers) to their home and pupate inside it. It is composed of many layers of silk stuck together with gum to form a thick material which requires a very sharp knife to make an opening in it. This, and not the rough fibre which covers the parchment or the silky thread that forms the little loosely woven cocoons inside the mass, is the Anaphe silk. The moth is pretty, of a cream colour, with lattice-work pattern of brown bars on the wings. The eggs have little yellow fluffy tufts on them, and look like minute velvet buttons.

There are two reasons why this silk has not a better place in the world's markets—for there is a great demand for all kinds of silk. One reason is that it has to be treated to get rid of the gum before it can be used, and the second is that mixed up with the cocoon's mass there is irritating fluff which is apt to get into the pores of the skin of anybody who handles it. No workman likes to get rashes on his hands, and cases of blood-poisoning have been known. It was thought that the caterpillars had so-called stinging hairs and left them in the nest-silk, but experiment showed that the caterpillars had straight hairs (not forked at the tip as those caterpillar hairs which produce rashes on sensitive skins and which are called stinging or poisonous), and it has now been discovered that the irritating fluff belongs to the *moths*, not to the caterpillars, and is scattered by them when they emerge.

Soaking the whole mass in strong soda and water, or subjecting it to heat to kill the moths before they emerge, makes it safe to handle. Some of these silk nests are very large, and may hold as many as three hundred cocoons. In some species there is no parchment cover, and these are of no value, because nothing can be made of the other material of the nests.

Some of the commonest of the Wild Silk Moths of North America can sometimes be bought from some of the London dealers in entomological specimens. They have been made familiar to us by Miss Gene Stratton-Porter in her delightful books *Moths of the Limberlost* and *The Girl of the Limberlost*, which contain very vivid descriptions of the life-histories of these moths in their own home, besides the thrilling adventures of their capture.

LAC INSECTS

Some of the beaked insects of this group have a very curious life, for at a certain period they get rid of all the organs they can possibly dispense with, retaining only those which actually keep them alive, and become mere gummy lumps, or scales, on the bark of twigs, to which they attach themselves by their beaks ; and thus they remain until the end of their existence—if this is worthy of being called an existence.

Some of these scale insects do a great deal of damage to the plants and trees they feed upon, where they establish themselves in enormous numbers, for no plant can long withstand their attack. Not only do they lessen its vitality by extracting fluid from its tissues, but the wounds they make give opportunity to the bacteria and fungus spores which are always present in the atmosphere, and the plant becomes diseased.

But there is one species of scale insect which has been discovered to be of commercial value, and instead of being checked is encouraged to increase, plants being cultivated on purpose for it to feed upon. This is the insect which produces a clear resinous substance known as lac and a deep red dye known as lac-dye.

The Lac Insect begins life as a quite active little red larva, about a thirtieth of an inch in length ; it runs about, and feeds by perforating rind or bark with its beak and sucking out the juices. Soon, however, it chooses a spot on which to settle, buries its beak in the tissues of a twig, and begins to manufacture in its body a gummy material, which oozes out of it and gradually covers it up, hardening in the air and forming a sort of shell covered with a white powdery substance which protects it from enemies. This is the scale, and the material of which it is composed is the famous lac.

The female settles down for life, loses all her organs, and becomes a tiny red sac with a beak, covered with a shell like a minute tortoise, except that from the part that used to be her thorax and where she should naturally carry wings tufts of hairs sprout and protrude through two holes in the scale ; from the end of her body there is another tuft which contains the ends of her breathing tubes ; these hairs are covered with a white powder, just as in the case of the scale. The red colour of the female is due to the liquid in her body, of which ultimately her eggs will be formed. This is the red lac-dye.

The male also makes a scale, but he does not remain imprisoned for ever ; he never dispenses with his eyes, and that fact, in addition to the shape of his scale, distinguishes him from the female. After a rest-period he emerges, with wings in the second generation, though the first is wingless.

The twigs on which lac insects are clustered are sold as raw material and known as *stick-lac*. The resin is then broken up, crushed, and washed in hot water to get rid of all the colouring matter, and is then known as *seed-lac*. After this it is melted and strained through thick canvas and spread out in thin layers ; this is the *shellac*, and in this form it reaches our country. It varies very much in colour, but the lighter the shade the higher is its value. Shellac may be bleached by being dissolved in boiling caustic potash and passing chlorine through the solution ; it is then called *white shellac*. The *lac-dye* is obtained by evaporating the water in which the *stick-lac* has been washed ; it is then sold in small squares, and is similar to cochineal.

India is the only country at present which makes an industry of lac production. Lac is obtained chiefly from the East Indies, Bengal, Siam, and Assam. It is used in various ways, being the principal ingredient of sealing wax and the basis of some varnishes. It is also used in the manufacture of gramophone records ; in the East Indies the natives make it into ornaments.

Sometimes it is obtained in large quantities, and at other times the season is bad, the enemies of the lac insects grow too strong for them, or there is some other reason why they do not multiply. Then, of course, lac is difficult to procure, and the price goes up, but no good substitute has yet been found for it.

COCHINEAL INSECTS

Cochineal dye is not used now, and the Cochineal Insects from which it is obtained are not cultivated any longer, but for many centuries it was very highly prized, because that particular colour, a beautiful rich carmine, could not be obtained by any other means. But when chemists discovered that a great variety of dyes could be produced from coal tar these manufactured dyes (aniline dyes) quite took the place of what are called natural dyes—that is, those which are made from plants such as madder or indigo, and the famous Tyrian purple dye of a certain shell-fish, and the dye of the Cochineal Insect.

The history of the Cochineal Insect is most curious and interesting, for at one time it was prized by crowned heads, bought at fabulous prices, quarrelled over by great men, and was even the innocent cause of bloodshed ; and then, after attaining the highest pinnacle of fame, it became quite worthless, all in a moment as it were, because of the discovery of a new method of producing dyes. Seven or eight hundred years ago it was cultivated to provide dyes for the robes of all the grandees of Europe, and to-day it has no higher use for mankind than that of keeping down certain weeds which used to be grown as its food.

Like the Lac Insect these little dye-producers are scale insects, and only move about when just hatched to find a suitable spot on which to settle down for life. Then they lose all their limbs and become tiny sacs of fluid, with very slender, hair-like beaks fixed into the tissues of the plant from which they get nourishment. They are natives of Mexico, where their food-plants are a certain species of cactus known to us as the prickly pear. The females alone have this red fluid, and are collected off the plants, and then killed with boiling water or steam or by exposing them to the sun. They are tiny insects ; it has been reckoned that 70,000 go to a pound !

From very remote ages the Mexicans had known and used this dye, and when the Spaniards conquered Mexico in the middle of the sixteenth century they found out what was being done, and began to cultivate the insect and its food-plant. Now the Spaniards saw in the Cochineal Insect a goose which should lay golden eggs for them, and they intended to keep this goose to themselves and make the whole world buy at their markets ; so all information as to how the insects were reared and how the dye was prepared was jealously guarded, very severe penalties, even the death sentence, being imposed upon anybody who let out the secret. So successfully were these restrictions carried out that, although the Spaniards introduced the insect into their own colonies and into Spain, no other country could find out anything about it, and the most absurd stories were invented, describing it sometimes as an animal and sometimes as a plant which produced this lovely colour.

One bold Frenchman who was governor of Dominica did manage with great difficulty to get hold of a " few feet of cochineal "—which means, of course, a strip of the plant with the insects attached—and a copy of the instructions for its welfare. He actually established the industry in Dominica in 1778, but he might have spared himself the trouble, for nothing would induce the settlers to see the advantage of cultivating these insects, and they allowed them to die out, and the precious documents were lost.

France at last got her chance in 1823, because in that year her troops were occupying Cadiz. A company of army surgeons were told off to obtain the Cochineal Insect at any cost and study its culture, and so successfully did they accomplish their task that in a few months they had got all the specimens and the information that was needed. One hundred and fifty mother Cochineal Insects made a triumphant voyage to the French island of Corsica in a special brig, and were established there and in the Royal Gardens at Paris.

Thus the industry became universal property, and flourished wherever the insects would live, and wherever it was introduced prickly pear nurseries were grown as food.

Then came the failure of the cochineal industry ; artificial

218

dyes could be produced much more cheaply, and with far more certainty, than by the rearing of insects, and so these were cultivated no more. But though it was easy to suspend its cultivation it was not so easy to get rid of its food. The prickly pear grew very luxuriantly in some countries where it was introduced, especially in Queensland and in South Africa. The most satisfactory means of coping with it now is to keep up supplies of the insects which feed on it, and so the only service the Cochineal Insect can render to man is to check the spread of the very plant which once was grown with such care as its food.

BEES

In very early days in the history of mankind it was discovered that bees could be made use of, and bee-keeping was understood even by uncivilized nations. Honey is popular as food all over the world—it does not need a highly cultivated taste to appreciate anything sweet—and even among the savage tribes of any country to-day where wild honey-bees are to be found there is always great competition to hunt down the colonies and get their honey-store.

The true hive-bees which man has domesticated are supposed to have originated in the countries bordering the Mediterranean, and both the Greeks and the Romans went in largely for bee-cultivation. In those days, of course, bees were valued for the sake of their honey only; nowadays we know that they are still more important to man because they accomplish the cross-fertilization of flowers, and fruit-growing depends entirely upon the successful pollination of the fruit-blossom. Thousands of hives are to be found in the fruit-growing counties of England ; the bee-keepers benefit by the rich supply of food for their bees, and the fruit-growers benefit by the visits of the bees, because without them there would be neither fruit nor blossom.

What the bees extract from the flowers is not honey—it is called nectar, and it undergoes a certain change before it becomes honey. The worker-bees collect nectar to feed the brood, and as they fly from flower to flower until they have sufficient it is carried in the crop or honey-bag inside the bee's body. Being mixed with saliva as the bee swallows it, it is changed into a digestible form for the young bees before it is stored in the cells for them. This is honey. It has a certain amount of nourishment, and can be used instead of sugar, so it is valuable as a food. The bee naturally stores it to feed the larvæ when there are no flowers to be found ; man has made use of this instinct, and gives the insects special cases to store in, then takes the honey for his own use, replacing it by sugar. If bee colonies are kept in a healthy condition and have plenty of opportunity for collecting nectar they will store large quantities of honey in any country which has a temperate climate. In warm countries, however, where there is never a time of scarcity in the matter of blossom, but plants can be found in bloom all the year through, the bee does not store more than sufficient for temporary needs, and the colonies are not very profitable to the bee-keepers. People have been very disappointed when they have given themselves a great deal of trouble in carrying queen-bees out to these countries, and establishing them, only to find after all their pains that by the second year the bees become demoralized by the abundance of food and will not make provision against a time of famine which never comes.

Besides honey beeswax is collected from the hives and sold for various purposes. The wax is the material used by the bees for building the cells which hold the honey and the brood. It is manufactured in the body of the workers, which at a certain time hang in clusters from the roof of the hive until the wax exudes from the under-surface of their body in the form of eight little flat flakes. Each bee, working in turn and in perfect order, makes the wax into a plaster in her mouth before beginning to build ; when her material comes to an end another bee takes her place and goes on with the work. Bees have to economize their wax, for the quantity they can produce is limited. It has been estimated that one bee must consume fifteen to twenty pounds of honey in order to produce one pound of wax.

The best candles are made of beeswax ; they are very firm, and do not burn so quickly nor gutter as those made from paraffin-wax are liable to do. The wax has to undergo several processes before it is ready to be made into candles. It is melted in boiling water, then collected again from the top of the water where it floats, strained, and to get rid of the yellow colour cut into thin ribbons, which are bleached in the sun.

CHAPTER XVIII

SOCIAL INSECTS

INSECTS soon discovered that it is an advantage to live together in numbers and share the duties of the community between them. There are some indeed which only make up sorts of family parties, and others live in clans or tribes, each individual living its own separate existence, but sharing a common dwelling. These cannot be called social insects, because by a society or community we mean a state where members are of use to one another and share the work, each being fitted to perform a particular task for the whole. And the members of such a community also share its privileges, for each is benefited by the work which is done by the other members.

A moment's reflection will show us that this system gives the best chance of development to the members which belong to it. How could we human beings, for example, find time to develop any special line of activity, such as a profession or a trade, if we had each to provide our own food, grow our own corn, bake our own bread, tan our own leather to make our own shoes, and so on? But by living together in a community each contributes some special work to the whole and also has time to devote to his special branch, and by practising that alone can bring it to the highest point of perfection of which he is capable.

222

Among insects, bees, wasps, and ants have adopted the social life, and among ants it has reached its highest development ; but those insects which merely live in company are

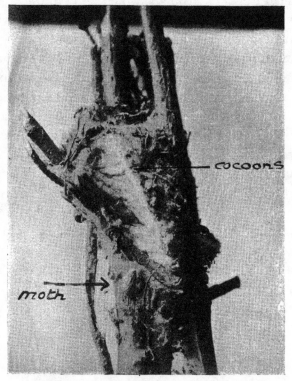

COCOONS OF A SMALL MOTH SPUN UP IN A COLONY

also worth studying, because in them we see the various steps which lead up to the marvellous communal system which is only practised by what we call social insects.

In several species of caterpillars a whole family will spin a web together and live inside it ; they do this as a protection

223

against enemies, and there does not seem any further advantage to be gained by thus living in company, except perhaps an economy of silk. Here in Britain we have several, such as the Small Egger caterpillars, which build quite large communal webs on hawthorn or sloe in the summer months. It is delightful to watch such a community growing up. When they want to feed they crawl out among the leaves, and come straggling back to the family web as their several appetites are appeased. A touch on the branch which holds them will make every caterpillar remain still in what looks like a listening attitude, and a vigorous shake will cause them to scramble out of the web and lower themselves hastily into the herbage on gossamer ropes in all directions, so that even if a large bird were to tear at the web, it would probably manage to catch only one or two at the most. The Lackey Moth caterpillars, Small Ermines, and some others lead the same kind of life while they are young, and separate when they reach the last stages of their larval life ; there are others which remain together even in the pupal stage. The African silkworms (*Anaphe*) do this, and many of the tiny moths which are called the *Micro-lepidoptera*.

There is a curious and interesting little insect, called Embia, which is found in tropical countries, and resembles an earwig without forceps. These insects weave wonderful tubes of silk and live side by side, using one another's galleries quite amiably, and no doubt finding safety from their enemies inside the webs.

The social system is developed a little further among certain tiny insects which feed together while they are young and have a queen-mother over them. Some of the gall-

224

dwelling aphids or plant-lice are among these. Most of
them are so minute that it is not easy to observe them, but
their life-history is very curious. There is a certain species
which forms a lovely little mauve or pink dwelling on the
leaves of elms, usually young trees ; some years it is in
such numbers that it can scarcely escape observation. *This*
gall is large enough and
conspicuous enough to
attract attention, but as a
rule they are quite small.

All these galls are
formed by the same
method ; the queen-
mother with her little
ovipositor manages to
deposit eggs in the tissue
of a plant just where
the growth of it may be

EMBIA, AND ITS SILKEN TUNNEL

checked. While a plant is growing it must have room to
expand, and if it be checked in one direction by these eggs
it must push out in another ; so a swelling is produced
on a leaf or stem, inside which the larvæ develop, the
queen-mother—who produces several generations—living
with them. The marvellous points about these galls are
their colours and shapes ; these vary according to the plant
they are formed upon, for the same species of plant-lice will
produce different structures on different plants, although
they all serve the same purpose whatever shape they may
be—that is, they supply a shelter for the whole family in the
early part of their lives, until they are ready to disperse.

All these insects are produced from one female, for only the last eggs that she lays at the end of the summer hatch out as females which are able to lay eggs in the next year. This is also the rule of the queens of the social insects which we will now consider.

NEST OF A SMALL WASP
Hugh Main

In all communities of social insects it is the queen who founds them. She has a very hard task, for she has to do all the work herself at first, choosing the site and planning the nest without any help. Then she lays a few eggs and watches over them until they hatch, after which she has to supply all the wants of the larvæ. One fancies that it must be a vast relief to her when the larvæ turn into pupæ, for they are such

226

helpless little things, but even then, when they are pupæ, they must still be watched, and tended, and helped out of their pupal envelope when they at last are ready to crawl out as mature workers. After that the queen is really a queen ; that is, she is waited upon by attendants and is not expected to do any work. The only thing required of her is to lay eggs—in fact she becomes nothing more than an egg-laying machine. In ant colonies the eggs are taken away by the workers as fast as they are laid ; in wasp and bee colonies the queen lays them in cells prepared for their reception. Bees have only one queen to each colony, but wasps, white ants (termites), and ants may have many queens in one nest.

As a rule the males do not meet with much kindness ; when once the mating season is over a male is of no further use to the community and only means an extra mouth to feed. Hive-bees actually turn out and kill their drones directly the honey-collecting season is over, but bumble-bees, wasps, and ants merely have nothing to do with their males, which wander about homeless and find shelter and food wherever they can until their short lives are finished. It is a very per-plexing condition of things that, whereas every female worker of the community, whether queen or worker, lives only for the next generation, the males have no interest whatever in any of the incidents which make up the daily life of the nest, and have nobody to consider except themselves ; so perhaps we need not waste much time in pitying them. Only among white ants (which are not true ants) does the queen's mate live with her, the royal couple occupying a cell in the centre of the nest.

The duties of the workers of the communities are very

varied in the different kinds of nests. Broadly speaking, they all have to collect material for the nest, collect food, usually store it, wait on the queen, rear the young, and guard the nest.

Hive-bee workers are rather mechanical in their method of working ; their instincts are so marvellous that they do not seem to need more than instinct to run their communities. Wasps show rather more intelligence over their work, pro-bably because they often have to use their wits over some unusual task which does not belong to the routine of their daily life. For instance, the collecting of the food which worker-wasps have to provide for the larvæ requires more exercise of their mental powers than does that of the nectar and pollen which bees have to bring home. The collecting of the latter does not require much learning, but wasps have to collect live insects, and that is quite a different matter. These have to be searched for most diligently, and any new hiding-place or cunning camouflage when once it is discovered must be remembered for future occasions, so that no time shall be wasted. Wasps have excellent memories, and seldom have to learn the same thing many times over. Bees have good memories, but on the whole wasps have even better ones. Memory seems to be one of the developments of the social insects. Flies, which have very highly developed organs, cannot be considered to have any memory of this kind ; they may have the same experience over and over again and yet learn nothing by it. A fly will return again and again to the same spot where a Praying Mantis sits wait-ing for it, and may have many narrow escapes, perhaps even be injured by the mantis, and yet return to be finally caught and devoured. But one experience of this kind is usually sufficient to teach a wasp or an ant.

Everything is arranged in a social nest to save as much time as possible. There is a great deal of work to get through, and a number of mouths to feed. Ants have still greater need to economize time, because they have to fetch all their provisions on foot, which must occupy very much more time than it would if they had wings like worker bees and wasps. The ants make sure that no precious moment shall be wasted, by sending out scouts in all directions to look for food, and when these meet with something which is too big for them to carry back alone they make an ant-path by laying a scent-trail to the spot. The path is made by the scout dragging her body flat along the ground, and with the first pair of legs pushing and scratching any loose soil, etc., which is in the way, at the same time putting out a strong-smelling fluid from her body. The result is a smooth road with a strong scent upon it ; and soon a long procession of workers will stream along it, some going forward, and others hurrying back with booty to the nest.

The soldier-ants—whether of the white ants or true ants —guard the nest by ceaseless patrollings, so that no enemy dare venture near. The soldier-ants of some tropical species have enormous heads quite out of proportion to the rest of their bodies, and a bite from them is something to be avoided, not only because of the size, but because of the formic acid they inject into the wound. Some species will squirt up this acid in a stream ; our largest British ants, the wood ants or horse ants, will go through this performance when their nest is disturbed or when they are unduly excited. On one occasion some of the soldier-ants on sentry-go for the colony in the Insect House (to which we have referred before) gave an exhibition of this feat. They threw themselves into an attitude in which the body was tucked under them and the head pointed straight up into the air. They then sent up a little jet of fluid quite three inches high. It has been recorded that this species can squirt these jets to a height of five inches, which is extraordinary when we consider their size. Soldier-ants of some tropical species squirt out an evil-smelling liquid which is a most effective weapon either in attack or defence. It is only among ants that certain individuals are set aside to defend the nest or conquer other colonies. Wasps and bees have no such division of labour, but the whole community of their workers combines to defend the nest if it is attacked, and, instead of patrolling, a sentinel is always on guard at the entrance to the nest so that nobody can take them unawares.

There is no doubt that the whole community benefits by thus dividing up the work of the colony among certain groups of workers. The slave-making ants, however, have gone quite crazy over this scheme of specialized labour, and have brought it to such a pitch that it is become an absurdity—at least according to human ideas. These ants steal larvæ and eggs of other species of ants to rear in their own nurseries that these may perform what we should consider the dullest and most menial tasks—though of course all work is equally important to the whole colony. These slave-ants have even to feed their masters as the larvæ are fed—that is, by making the food into a sort of pap in their own mouths first. This curious custom must have been carried out by very many generations, because now, in these days, the masters are quite unable to feed themselves, and rely entirely on their slaves to keep them alive. They seem to have somehow lost the necessary sense-organs which direct the preliminary actions of eating, because even with food within reach they will slowly starve to death unless their slaves are there to present it to them in a predigested form. This seems to us to be carrying specialized labour to ridiculous lengths, yet it is probable that the development of this astonishing system is of some advantage to the ants which practise it, because this particular group, the slave-makers, are reckoned to be the most intelligent of all ants.

Much remains to be said about the delightful habits of the various kinds of ants and the astounding work which is carried out by some species, but all this must be left to a future volume, for this chapter merely deals with the systems of all social insects and the duties of the members of the various communities.

Bumble-bees (or humble-bees) have a different system of working their colonies from that of ants or of hive-bees. Indeed, it is far more like a family than a colony, for the queen-mother shares nearly all the duties of the workers. Bumble-bees are very gentle, sweet-tempered creatures, and the beautiful devotion of the queen bumble-bee to her brood all through her life is quite in accordance with her character, and is very far removed from the part which other queen insects play in their domestic life. This queen-mother never becomes a mere egg-laying machine like the queens of ants, wasps, and hive-bees, but to the end of her busy life, until she is too weak and old to work any longer, she flies out in the morning like the rest of the workers, and collects pollen and nectar for the brood whenever she is not engaged in laying eggs. She is very independent for a queen, and has no attendants to feed her and wait upon her ; she combs out her own shaggy coat and keeps herself smart without any assistance. Moreover, the duty devolves upon her to keep order in her own household, for at times the workers may be unruly and try to tamper with the brood.

The young queen bumble-bee comes out of her winter quarters in the spring and chooses a suitable site for a nest. This is usually a hole in the ground, but some species prefer more romantic places. It is not unusual to find an old bird's nest occupied by bumble-bees ; the cosy, moss-lined, domed nests of wrens and chiff-chaffs are much to their taste, or an old mouse's nest, which is lined with grass. A ready-made lining saves time, of course, but the queen can collect bits of grass, moss, or dead leaves herself if necessary. She next collects pollen, which she works into a paste, moistening it with her mouth and mixing it with nectar. A lump of this is put on the floor of the nest, and a tiny cell of wax is formed in the middle of it after much kneading and shaping with her jaws. In this cell the first little batch of eggs is laid and sealed over with wax. After this work provision for the larvæ has to be gathered in, and also for herself in case of bad weather. So the queen sets to work to make a honey-pot, which she keeps brimful whenever the weather is not too cold or rainy to collect the nectar. When she is not collecting nectar she is incubating her eggs, for she actually hatches them herself, sitting on them as a hen does, and covering them with her furry coat as a hen covers the eggs with her feathers. She spends a great deal of her time doing this, stretching out her tongue to the honey-pot when she is hungry. As soon as the little larvæ hatch out the careful mother seals them over again with wax. She feeds them herself with a mixture of honey and pollen from her mouth, and every time a meal-time comes round she has to bite a little hole in their wax ceiling to get at them, and seal it again when she has finished. The floor of their nursery (into which they burrow) also provides them with food ; it is the original lump of pollen mixture—bee-bread—which the queen-mother first put down for them. When the larvæ pupate they each form a tough cocoon ; the wax covering is now cleared away, as they are well protected, so that the queen can stretch herself on the cocoons. For the warmth of her body is necessary to bring out the young bees, and the greater part of the queen's day is taken up by this work. This duty she does not even forgo when the workers emerge and can help her with the rearing.

Toward the end of the summer the queen lays eggs which develop into males and females to carry on new colonies in the following year. The males or drones do not return to the nest after pairing is over, but the young queens often linger there as if loath to quit the home nest, and even forget their royal dignity so far as to collect pollen like the workers. But when colder weather sets in they all disperse, and may be seen crawling about and peering into holes and crevices until they are satisfied with some warm, dry corner into which they may creep for their winter sleep. But the queen-mother grows gradually weaker and weaker until she dies, and those workers which may be still vigorous will not live long without her. So the happy family breaks up, and the nest is left deserted, with perhaps a few larvæ or pupæ which soon perish from lack of attention.

Young queen wasps also hibernate and form the new

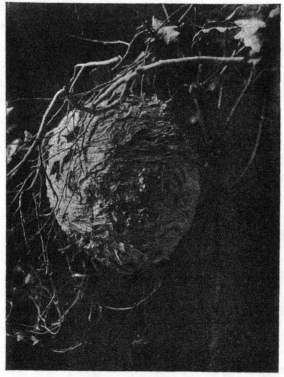

NEST OF TREE WASP

colony in the spring. We have two groups of wasps in Britain ; in both groups the nest is beautiful, manufactured out of bits of wood or plants or fibre, etc., chewed into a pulp and then flattened out into ribbons with the jaws and first pair of legs. This forms the outer envelope of the nest inside which the combs are built. It is impossible, of course, to see this beautiful structure in the underground nests of Ground Wasps, but nests of the Tree Wasp are built in trees or bushes, often in gooseberry bushes, and then all the operation connected with building and repairing can be easily observed, and a truly delightful study it is.

The life-history of the wasps resembles that of bumble-bees. The queen hibernates until spring days are warm enough to bring her out of her winter quarters. All alone she starts the paper envelope which is to be the home of the future colony. She does not carry the work very far, but builds a little cone (which will eventually be the top of the nest—sufficiently large to cover a few cells, in which she lays eggs. When these hatch she has to tend the larvæ herself until they pupate and emerge as young worker-wasps. But after this she leaves all the work of the colony to them and gives her time to egg-laying. She is a true queen inasmuch as her subjects depend upon her, and if she should die and there were no young queen to succeed her the worker-wasps would soon quit their labours and not even feed, and the colony would die out. But she does not take any other part in the work, so she becomes a mere egg-laying machine, like the queens of ants and white ants.

The little stingless bees which are found in warm countries also live in colonies. They make their nests among the branches or in the trunks of trees, building them up of material very like that used by bumble-bees. Their honey-pots are suspended in irregular-shaped cells, in which they are fastened by slender shafts of wax. Species of this group appear to have one queen, but the number of workers in a colony is comparatively large.

235

The largest communities resulting from one queen are those of white ants—or Termites—whose queens are said to lay 30,000,000 eggs in their lifetime ! The queen lives in

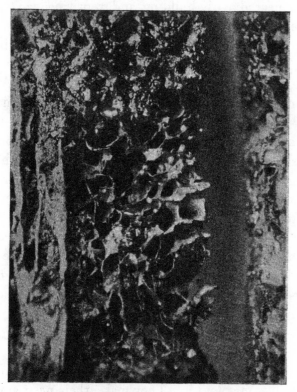

CELLS IN A NEST OF STINGLESS BEES

a cell in the centre of the nest, in which she is a prisoner. Because of her enormous size she almost fills this cell, and cannot get through the passages by which the workers reach her. She is waited upon entirely by them, and as fast as she lays the eggs they are carried away to the nurseries to be hatched. A most curious point about the social system of white ants is that if necessary a worker may be turned into a queen to suit the needs of the colony. From experiments

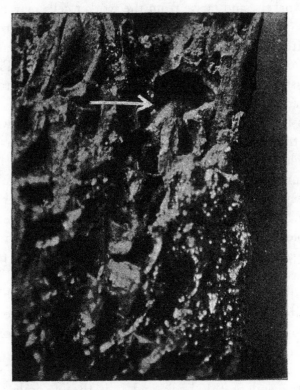

HONEY-POTS OF STINGLESS BEES

on hive-bees it has been discovered that those bee larvæ which are to become queens must be fed on certain food called royal jelly, and that if the larvæ which would normally become workers are fed on this special diet they will emerge as queens. It is true that in the nest the royal cells are

237

larger than the worker cells, but the eggs are exactly the same size, and the larger cell is simply to allow for the larger growth of the royal larva. Larvæ from royal cells may grow up as workers, and larvæ from the worker cells may become queens, by changing their diet; but among white ants, even after they have emerged from the pupal state, a worker may become a queen by being fed on royal diet. This is a really astounding fact, and comes as a great surprise to those who learn it for the first time.

This leads me to conclude with some words of warning which the reader must accept patiently, knowing that they are for his own good.

In our studies of insects it is always necessary to cultivate and keep an open mind. It is useless to consider when we are faced with some point that because it is very improbable therefore it must be impossible and not worth investigating. And although it is very important to read up all we can find about any insect we are interested in, yet we must remember all the time that it is quite possible that the writers have made mistakes. Therefore if there is any opportunity of doing so we should test the truth of their statements before taking anything for granted.

One more word of warning must be added before we reach the end of this book, and it is that no collection of insects should be made without accompanying notes of the life-history of each specimen.

This sounds perhaps as if I wanted to turn a hobby into an irksome study, but it is nothing of the kind. I have been shown lately two cabinets, belonging to two types of boy naturalists, which will illustrate exactly my meaning. The first was a magnificent collection of insects of which anyone might well be proud : beautiful tropical butterflies and moths, large or brightly coloured beetles, gauzy-winged dragonflies, etc. But when the owner exhibited the specimens he had no interesting information to give about any one of them. Some had been bought from dealers in the City ; others had been presented by friends and relatives ; quite a number had been collected by uncles in " different parts of the world " —he was even hazy as to what countries they belonged to ! About half a dozen were British butterflies which he had himself caught in the New Forest, but these were not named, nor did he know the caterpillars of those species. It was really rather a sad collection, although the specimens were so beautiful, because one felt that an enormous amount of pleasure had been missed for lack of an intelligent interest. But I do believe that not many boy owners would be content with the mere possession of what should have been a fund of deep enjoyment.

The second collection was not an unusual one ; I have seen many such, and have always had much pleasure from them. It was of British insects arranged in groups, with the date of capture and the name of the place on neat little labels. With the collection was a diary of all sorts of odd little notes about the specimens, chiefly the owner's own observations. All the specimens were named, even the quite tiny moths ; those names which could not be found out from books or from the exhibition cases in the Natural History Museum had been supplied by the kind folk in the Insect Room under that museum. That boy loved his collection of insects more than anything else he possessed, because he had bred out every specimen himself. He knew each specimen individually, and something of its habits. This surely is the right way to make a collection, for a diary or a book of notes adds enormously to its value.

And lastly for those who are keen to read up facts for themselves the following books are delightful and are full of interesting information : *The Girl of the Limberlost* and *Moths of the Limberlost*, by Gene Stratton-Porter ; *Aquatic Insects*, by Professor Miall ; *Wasps : Social and Solitary*, by G. W. and E. G. Peckham ; *Ants*, by A. Forel ; and *Pond Life*, by Edwin C. Ash.

INDEX

INDEX

Touch, sense of, 139
Trachæ, 113
Tropical countries appreciated by insects, 47, 48 ; butterflies in, 83, 87 ; moths in, 87 ; Praying Mantis in, 48
Tsetse Fly, 188–9

'Useful' insects, bees, 219, 221 ; Blister Beetle, 75 ; cochineal, 216–219 ; silkworms, 202–13

'Vanishing,' 51
Vapourer Moth, 161
Variation in insects, 34–50
Veins, arrangement of, 127 ; importance of, in identification of insects, 127
Vision, sense of, 105, 106
Volucella, 81

Wasps, 72, 228 ; colonies of, 227 ; fossil forms of, 43 ; memory of, 141 ; nests of, 234 ; parasitic, 55, 58, 132 ; stings of, 131, 133 ; wing-adjustment of, 123
Water-beetle, 114
Water Scorpion, 120
White Butterfly, 129
White shellac, 215
Wild Silk Moth, 132, 210, 213
Wing-lobes of grasshopper, 26
Wings, 121 ; action of, in flying, 127–30 ; wing-buds, 122, 126 ; patterns on, 82 ; rate of motion of, 128, 129 ; shape of, 130 ; uses and power of, 121–35 ; wing-cases, 97
Wood Wasp, 184
Woodlice, 42

Yucca Moth, 197

Zoological Gardens of London, 81, 143, 230

CPSIA information can be obtained
at www.ICGtesting.com
Printed in the USA
BVHW031154201220
596125BV00016B/197